THE LEAVES ARE
SOMETHING THIS YEAR

OTHER WORK
BY ED BARRETT

Poetry

The Sinatra n
Toward Blue Peninsula
Down New Utrecht Avenue
Bosston
Kevin White
Rub Out
Sheepshead Bay
Practical Lullabies for Joe (collaboration with Joseph Torra)
Common Preludes

Chapbooks

Or Current Resident
Breezy Point
Theory of Transportation

Poetry/Mixed Media Collaborations

Meadowsweet (text and drawing, with Michael Russem)
And when it sank to eye level (text, acrylic paint on vellum,
with Eung-Sun Lee)
Tideline (text, oil paint on vellum, with Grace Coletta)
Holy Sonnets (text, wood, ceramics, linen, with
Amanda Matthews)

Translations

Antigone

THE LEAVES ARE
SOMETHING THIS YEAR

New and Selected Prose Poems

1994–2022

ED BARRETT

Quale Press

Acknowledgments

To my publishers at Groundwater Press, *lift*, Quale Press, Zoland Books and Pressed Wafer, how can a simple thank you for your encouragement and support ever be enough?

William Corbett's friendship; his enthusiasm for publishing my work at Pressed Wafer; our Friday afternoons at the Grafton Street pub talking about the Red Sox, poetry and movies; his postcards and letters brimming with life and laughter....

To the editors of the journals and magazines where versions of many of these poems first appeared, thank you for welcoming me in.

To Joe Torra, Ann Lauterbach, Don Berger, John Ashbery, Michael Franco, Jim Behrle, Christopher Sawyer-Lauçanno, Patricia Pruitt, Roland Pease, Martha Collins, and Charles North, thank you for your kind responses over the years.

Do John Kennedy agus Áine Moynihan agus Feargal MacAmhlaoibh, go raibh maith agaibh.

COVER AND INTERIOR DESIGN | ALEX GREULICH

for Liam Barrett

and

in memory William Corbett

CONTENTS

from **The Boston Trilogy**

Viking Renga (2022)

from COMMON PRELUDES

(1994)

SONNET

1.

The graffiti should read *sweep my hair back gently, leaving the cornice its question of light.* If you understand anything about the way we live now, you know how the plot thinned out, the orange peel slides off in one of those perfect citrus spirals, our stare more serious than we let on. Columns of traffic in midtown wait like an intentional misgiving whose tears are iron in place of the god unaccustomed to grief. His children don't live forever and for this he blames them, for this he fashions riddles and labyrinths to keep them occupied until the mouse gnawing at the baseboard triggers a secret spring and the wall flies open and the shield and a tank-top (a little tight, a little skimpy) are revealed.

2.

Summer accumulated in a series of private lines and bee-stings, flesh reddening and peeling like a clock. Constant repair taught the blue and white harbor how pure an event thought was. Perfection was there, disguised as imperfection. Loss was disguised as abundance, to which there was no answering except normally, as if sheer presence sent a shock you could afterwards appoint notes to, neither aggrieved nor congruent, but another surface which threw you into history simply because you replied.

3.

The green swirl of light, off-center behind a ridge of pines not immersed in darkness but somehow giving that off like a hollow sun. My head is not seen, just as the pines really are there, just not visible in the wedge-shaped dark that intersects the distance to make this the foreground—"this" being where we stand (you are not seen too, so this isn't a self-portrait by any means)—neither one of us looking at the swirling light or the pines and the dark rising out of them: "this" is not a self-documenting universe but an applied chance that tugs at the longstanding yet abrupt sense that it would continue when you weren't there—would continue *because* you weren't there, marking by cadence the having it at all.

4.

That ham and cheese sandwich was delicious. A moment ago I was worrying about something (how we live now is to worry about something, usually one big thing) until I wasn't worrying about it and instead I was thinking about you and that funny half-light I see when I look at you. Part of this island has death written over it a thousand times, part lime juice and salt, part a custom-made sailor's jacket with gold piping across the breast—an essay in the form of a blazer—so that when you turn your head to the side like that, this is holding you here.

THEORY OF TRANSPORTATION

The ones we like stay later than the rest. The snow has already changed from early evening airmail envelope blue to crisp business letter white. In contrast, the sky is the kind of black before night goes brilliant again with reflected light from apartments and street lamps, constellations, the moon and other planets you could identify. This is the first part of night sprouting with haphazardly grouped numerals raised to this or that power: a line of trees or an arm raised in some gesture. Like trying to answer all the questions at the end of a chapter in a textbook: Wasn't it just a while ago we were reading the preface with so much understanding? How did these things come to stand for so much? It isn't as if we were in the front row of an amphitheater looking back on other rows of seats with numbers painted on them. That would be easy. Or even those constellations, once you get the hang of finding them: trunk of a horse (Pegasus) or the Big W (Cassiopeia)—a knack, like making snowballs, and immensely satisfying, as if nature were redeemable because constant, aloof, yet right there to squish between your fingers if you want to get close to it, if you think that might help. A line of trees or an arm raised in a gesture: pine trees stoop lightly in the wind, the arm curves up and out. You might think about what stance to take at such a moment. Perhaps the radiance of your room, lit with such simple truths as table and chairs, key-rings and painted wood can help. Testimony of friends and those who love you—won't that count? Won't that let them know what you were really up to? Happiness, I can assure you, is this: to be let off the hook a couple of times. It shows you how to treat others, a nonchalance that mounts to a delectable but nonetheless rigorous morality: your father who loved to fish but always threw his catch back in. Too bad he didn't treat his family with the same detached amusement. Either you wander around looking for something larger-than-life to be your life, or you marvel at waistcoats and thick brocade for their splendor and mystery. No, I'm not pretending there aren't important issues to discuss, crucial philosophical movements that arrange our minds for the moment the way a snowstorm arranges a city. Nor do I want to suggest that we can pretend to be "above the fray"—the hook I want to let you off of is made of steel: it has barbs to stick in the soft lining of your throat and not let go. Some don't get off—the ground we've already covered too predictable even if the numbers are astronomical and we can't count that high. Somebody, or something else, can; somebody or something else is those numbers, and we are too, but their telling hangs thick as knotted rope, thick as Welsh coal-mining songs. What would you do? What would you like to do? These questions get answered and an atmosphere condenses out of them, brilliant where you want it to be brilliant, dark chocolate where that makes sense, the raspberry lining of a jacket always a surprise. Even in this atmosphere, where love can sort it all out, the narrative is unflinching, grinding particulars into a kind of paste. An arm is not a good model for a tree.

I was saying it was getting dark out. People are starting to come home from work and lights go on in apartments up and down the block. Can I give you this? Can I say people are coming home from work and lights are going on in apartments up and down the block? No one can do that. I cannot keep you from disappearing again. I cannot say each light places its asterisk in the window to plead a special case, some exception.

SECRET TAPES

You just know how they will be able to show us it was serially encoded, conforming to a "current" of events like the Gulf Stream, in effect warming us to a love for the just city, meanwhile overlooking others in a fate which is cold and crushing and as surprisingly unsurprising as the tide of shoppers in the checkout aisle where everyone looks pursued by some Fury or other, stony-faced, like high school geography teachers. Ignorance is our own and others' problem, and the truth is much truer really, but I don't want to go into that now unless you want me to because the tokens of recognition by which we will learn from each other are as mysteriously funny as European telephone numbers or an address in Queens. I can say a true thing like a false one, and a false one like it was the truth, but also a true thing like the truth. The gates to the Academy of the Future of the Just City have already been closed behind us, gliding effortlessly on their hinges of ice and falling snow, with bars like sluices for the present to keep slopping in on us, a memory of what else is endured alone.

THE LEAVES ARE SOMETHING THIS YEAR

1.

It makes you think when you see it spread at your feet like a magic carpet. If I could speak the language of things, in every description I would be asking, *Do you have this?* Or, *Can I give you this?* It would say how much I loved you. It would be a charm to protect you. And since it is a small thing, it will go unnoticed, you will go unnoticed, although I could look now and then and see what I guess we knew all along, expecting our knowledge or expectations would add up to something, wouldn't only be added on to fall off just because they do that.

2.

Shadowing this is a second set of books where the real accounts are kept: an invisible arithmetic in long rows, some numbers so thick they look like squirrels running up trunks of trees with horse chestnuts in their mouths. They know. They know ordinary methods are best, hammered out of the giant age, the age of giants, which came after the age of smaller things, and before this one, which is called the age of squirrels who know best. Children and methods are buried in the ground. Do you want to say *so much*? Do you want to say *so much* as if it were your fate, one hand raised to the forehead, brushing back a wave of hair?

3.

Sometimes I think I can keep myself away from you and that it will be less trouble. Or even if I'm there, just not want you so much, in the way of not getting too attached because it's ultimately less painful, because there's no clarity of perception to cut through the invisible braid of desire. You turn your hand over and I kiss your shining wrist, exempt from everything that does not have this mark. And I claim this. Tomorrow, last year, have this geography. What can I give you?

4.

You are supposed to be going somewhere, in the sense of developing and incorporating the different things that happen into who you are, deriving yourself like an equation, factoring in the x's and y's, where x equals any discontinuous fragment of memory so strong it makes you feel like you're still there trying to figure out what it was for, and y that you are the one thing that will not translate into the purposely obscure text invented for it. Good, let it be like that, in the sense that what continued was the continuing part, and these other events, some of the people or things you keep thinking about, that just seem to have stopped, you don't get to revisit, and they don't exactly come back, but something in-between seems to be operating, where you don't make sense of it, with the feeling there are underground labyrinths and life on other planets. The leaves are really something this year: Vermonters where I go say they haven't seen color like this for a long time. In Corbett's top floor study there's a small volume of poems I wrote. Each time you think the clarity will come through and part of the secret will be eaten like cake. Each time you think this definitely has something to do with it.

5.

Here are these big things, like fate and attraction, looking the way they do, holding our lives to a standard of anguish and loss and elation. I don't think there's any escape from all of this: subtracting and subtracting until the only thing you see is what you were going to see. The interim could make you go the stoic route, a kind of balancing act of one absence (pain) over another (happiness), but I don't get that, even with my lifelong predisposition to the classics. Basically, I don't think we are classic: we want a real test with right and wrong answers when we step up to the examining table and have our lute and fireman's hat taken away. I want a philosophy that is pure description, weaving the fabric into just the way it looks. A disappearing act, the closer I get to it, and the coin shooting straight up my sleeve.

6.

My friend said she didn't think women fear contingency as much as just items in a series, a continual inventory that didn't go anywhere. To which I said some men don't say anything, bringing an absence in the hope that a woman will fill in the blanks, give them a kind of self-knowledge by default as if they had to be forced into recognizing what they were doing by having this audience to do it in front of. Not that I don't think public gestures count, or that, say, the death of the age of monumentality is necessarily a good thing. I can still imagine sculpture as a noble art—the age of irony won't work in a journal of the plague years—the unyielding made plastic and expressive, bronze apples rolling out in front of you, looking like they could still be soft at the center, like a sicko could hide razor blades inside them on Halloween. We live with these things. We live with our understanding of these things, like a character to whom the wizard says *This is a magic torch*, and the next day another wizard says *This is a magic torch as well*.

ESSAYS FOR THE MOMENT

1.

How they presented themselves, with such airs! You don't know anything if you don't know me, each of them seemed to say. So, the bronze ladder, rungs burnished a pale beer color where other hands and feet had climbed, was put aside. No, you would never forget what was important, falling asleep on the dunce's stool, awakening to moonlight tracing chalk on the floor of the abandoned schoolroom.

2.

You visit the colonial inn of your birthday and all the "atmosphere" vanishes: the smoky mirrors, the pleasant crush at the tavern's bar, platters of meat set out before the roisterers. The only one standing there out of costume is you, as you begin to attract attention and try to slow this process down because once the tavern's customers turn to look at you, they mysteriously disappear, leaving you standing in a re-creation of the same exact scene, only it's in a mall, a place you never wanted to go to, but now that you've been there a couple of times you're used to it—besides it's the kind of place you think you can stop going to without missing anything. "Spats" it's called and there's a fake musket hanging on one wall and huge copper pots on another. Some of the businessmen drink vodka gimlets, some are having Dewars on the rocks. The bartender feeds you a line, then retreats into the darkness as if you were about to embark upon a set speech that has become famous and studied in all the schools because it is one of those statements of a grand theme that we will explore in the next few weeks and I don't think we will get any answers but we can ask a few questions that will make us think, and this is material you will have to know for the exam anyway. It's your birthday, so enjoy—only it's really the myth of Narcissus you are entering, a metamorphosis which is not the final one, only the next in a series of continually evolving scene changes mounted like a dream. The barroom goes dark; the actor is frozen, facing the audience. A single spot picks him out. He speaks: "I see that my real business is elsewhere, right here beside me, and that I have been carrying around this weight of grief and joy like two gym bags with their shoulder straps dragging along the ground. I feel like I still have them, but with a good shrug I can balance them, so that I'm standing here with a firm grip on the handles, and there is this pleasant sensation of my arms being pulled straight down my sides. I know it'll change soon as I start walking—I'll have to move, you can't stand still in the middle of such a busy street without attracting attention—but this moment of reflection is enough to get me through the thoughtless, chafing hours I wear like a suit of toxic side-effects. I don't mind. But why the oppression of certain visitations, so that the whole day is like this: a sense of loss but without regret, just a question about what it means now that I'm feeling it—a presence, like the gun-metal disc of a storm moving up the coast, still many miles out to sea, coiled like an eye that is about to look at something, not just reflect the mantle of fallen leaves? I've got it and I want to keep it, so here, take it. It'll go anyway, and if I don't try to hold on to anything, I won't spoil it for the next time."

3.

Then all these periods held domain and, like disco, were swallowed in turn by the earth which had given them life. Even the house was infested and burned, shrieking, to the ground. Tender love, sings the serial killer during recreation-time at the state hospital, tender love is the glue that holds it all together, someone's favorite dog racing across the lawn, right into the horn-of-plenty's maw. So, marks on the chalkboard began to crystallize on the floor of the ice arena. What will take contagion from our time? But there will always be queer, Scottish things (for example) that fascinate us with a sense of urgency. We know, and in this knowledge cannot keep the facts straight very long, which allows the *Niña*, the *Pinta*, and the *Santa Maria* to slip through the maelstrom like upside-down hats pulled across on wires, pronouncing clarity on all who live here. There will come a time—but that isn't something we should talk about since everything will be different then. Something immortal is a good way to preserve your impressions and desires, and everyone you love, to keep them out of harm's way, yet with the know-how and wherewithal to let them adapt to new things, so some kid doesn't shout, *Hey Methuselah, nice donkey-cart*, when you drive up to the front of your house. No one expected it to last very long, but we're paying for it into the next century, not too far away, coming towards us with its bagpipes and its kilt.

THE TRUE STORY

The true story makes it abundantly clear long after those diverting tales about the invention of cheese and silk panties, or the humdrum life of giants in Giantville, and how the pilgrims made their long journey to bring one surface in contact with another surface, like two pages facing each other in a book, with the interest more in the passage from one place to the other and all the changes of light and suffering on the voyage, the kinds of tunes they played on their tin whistles, what dances, the shape of their hats and shoe buckles, just the way our own passages from one state, say, of happiness to another, say, of "dejection: an ode" are more interesting, more fraught with danger than just showing up at the amphitheater. Definitions are casually thrown in (short-sword: a sword with a short blade) or "details on the whole are usually concrete," and facts from biology (vulva) as well as James Clerk Maxwell's field equation dealing with potential (the electrical kind) until the whole thing rounds itself out into a sort of promontory or island where we stand, very small and very distinct, staring out into all that blue, surprised at the amount of affection we feel for it today as we realize how good it is not to be the first ones here having to make up words for love or songs for jumping rope because there are prerogatives, after all, in heritage and chromosomes and history pulsing at our feet in little blue waves by the shore. It really is just today, like many another day in Evening Land where the action of the story is now taking place, although action is hardly the word for this exquisite moment since it doesn't matter whether we get it right or wrong; in fact, we're supposed to fail. Our pleasure is in watching them sink out there in the oriental surf, with the "full" knowledge that our turn may be next—although it never is our turn because when it comes, it's different. History is all around us in the shrouds of the parachute, and it's serious this business of ours, interlinearity, writing glosses on the violet-blue text of seeming. The brain turns around in its skull-pan, or the ear is trumpet for the neck. Flowers have been roaring out their names for the sky since early this morning. Each asterisk takes off like a helicopter buzzing the inhabitants of the cove down there who are waving or water-skiing behind their speedboats. What are their names for it? The textual commentator labels it a *locus classicus* and corrects the spelling. At least three doctors have been collecting footnotes on my own corpus in the hope of expunging errors and bringing out a corrected text. And someday they will too, but by then the barbarians will have sacked not only the provinces but also the capital, disfiguring all the statues, and the story will have passed to other hands who will carefully pack it with the two "o's": oblivion and obliquity. The surface really is a surface this time, receding just at the point where you want to enter it—the silver screen made out of mercury I think—although people and things are always disappearing behind it, and although these wonderfully large animal eyes stare back out at you.

ODEON

Soon as you see someone in a cab at night you want to look at them basically because of the drama of something shiny in the dark like a yellow taxi, the way skylines are very nice to look at, or of course those more fundamental kinds of skyline, constellations, which form an end to our way of thinking. The city is a kind of constellation if you want to get fancy: picture a map of the U.S. in the dark with the major cities against it with all their lights on. I like that: this is "Chicago" instead of a useless Greek mythological reference which does express a truth about something, but to so few. New York. And these would be new references which have already been well established but which are still surprising and disgusting as I imagine various myths must have been since they rarely mention disease except as plague, which is a legality. The lesson was that it was supposed to be condign: the same yellow school bus with one face pressed against the window and attendance being kept—or pain is very dark but will be light-filled, not this limestone daylight which cuts across our hands, but the light which both of us love when it fails innumerably throughout the city.

TRIPOLINE

The ultimate opera begins with an overture to Paris and Detroit. The music of this overture is two characters (one called "Paris," the other "Detroit") talking about these two capitals representing the poles between which all life occurs. Paris and Detroit have this conversation on a desert island surrounded by the bluest of blue water, a palm tree between them, and in the distance, faint smoke from a steamship that will soon rescue them. Paris mistakenly pronounces Detroit's name as "daytwa." Paris is dressed in a velvet painter's smock, the kind they don't make any more judging from the painters I know; he also wears a beret. Detroit, in honor of that city's past, is played by a full-sized car, or if that is not possible, by a glove compartment, or merely a glove. Act One is a single aria sung offstage by the heroine. She sings about her life, which doesn't seem all that marvelous or different, but it does make her sing. There's the slightest hint that if she doesn't sing the ordinariness will turn sour, though now it is not. The aria is written in Italian and Irish. It is called simply "Aria" or, in Irish, *Aria*. The classical unities are given a nod now and then, but this one-acter is more like a kiss.

NINE ACTS THAT WOULD HAVE KILLED VAUDEVILLE

1.

Two men in checkered flannel shirts, stage right; center stage, bow of ocean liner under construction. Lunch whistle. Shadow of bird glides across hull.

2.

Jack, a six-foot puppet, opens apartment window and steps onto fire escape. City noises below—faint, joyous. Jack, in red plaid shirt and jeans, is a dishwasher by day. Late summer night, still hot and muggy. He leans on fire escape railing, then sits on bottom step of a ladder leading to floor above. He rises, leans on fire escape again. Jack sings to the moon and the stars then retires for the evening. He sings about his job as a dishwasher, he sings about some times in the morning that he likes a lot, about late afternoon and friends he has. The moon, so taken by his song, and the Pleiades also, come down to his fire escape. The Pleiades spin rapidly around the moon (it is a crescent moon).

3.

Ink well, stage left. Stage right, nib of fountain pen enters. Sound of heavy rain.

4.

Fishermen, stern of ocean trawler. They wear bright yellow storm-pants with yellow suspenders. Crackle of radio in background. They haul in net glistening with fish. Stage left, lights come up to reveal a tableau vivant: *Czarina Elizaveta Petrovna Receiving Russia from the Hands of Her Dying Father, Peter the Great.*

5.

Forest ranger, lonely outpost of national park. Midnight. Strange light accompanied by "other-world" sounds. Scene changes: Longfellow House, Brattle Street, Cambridge, Massachusetts. Main sitting room, Longfellow memorabilia prominently displayed. Same light, sounds as before. Memorabilia begin to shake.

6.

Tom-toms. Large coffee (really large, about seven feet high, one of those take-out containers with a generic Greek frieze running around the sides), milk no sugar, descends center stage. Tom-toms continue until coffee touches stage, then silence, stage goes dark.

7.

Henry Wadsworth Longfellow, age seventeen, enters stage right, clothes torn, face bloodied, carrying soul of defeated alien from another world, which before it departs to its own notion of Paradise, bestows gift of poetical powers on young Hank. He begins reciting *The Song of Hiawatha*.

8.

Stage dark. Sound of subway train rumbling through tunnel; comes to stop. Sound of train doors opening and closing; sound of train departing. Light comes up to reveal Times Square Station, 3 a.m. Groups of homeless people barely visible, asleep in corners of station. Slowly, a man identified only as "City Official" descends stairs, stage right, and from deep inside his coat pulls out bucket of gold coins which he begins to pour into sleeping man's pockets. City Official backs away, and from stage left a shaft of radiant light, parallel to plane of stage, bathes his surprised and happy face. Shaft of light disappears causing momentary confusion and doubt, then reappears. This action repeats many times until City Official, perplexed, exits. Stage cleared, light continues to shine then disappear.

9.

Henry Wadsworth Longfellow, near death, is carried aboard waiting spaceship.

from SHEEPSHEAD BAY

(2001)

THE SONNETEER

I have surveilled this region day and night and still no trace of you. I must have been crazy buying reconnaissance software called The Sonneteer ("Because Life Is A Lesson In Grammar, A Series Of Endings!" "Direct Matters With Surprising Affection, Almost A Kind Of Knowledge About Life and Death, Dreaded As Thou Art!"). It offered to reach into the cone-shaped throat of darkness with my voice as through the surface of a stream, like a child trying to get at a shiny stone. Even the stars were warm and trashy; memory, my portion of recognition fated to be in there ("If Something Turns Into Something Else, Wasn't It Always That?"), inevitable and just as the Harry Warren tune "You'll Never Know" in which love parted its lips and sang *if you don't know now*.

GOETHE DID NOT INVENT
PHYSICS TO MURDER ANYONE

Goethe did not invent physics to murder anyone, and my memory crosses near him to place a very pretty plum-colored scarf around your neck as if it were a cravat, or even just the notion that we would say cravat. Goethe emerges in his "Theory of Colors" in German with the curve of the mountain road paring the apple of distance or emulation or sex (the scarf, let me remind you) of its skin until, just a little bit farther on, it twists into the sweetest little parish. Did you ever see such a pretty place? And just look who's coming out to say hello! In the scarf a purely German physical tumult, soft as the figures on the skin of a plum, the ghostly part is on fire. Hello, they say, hel-lo, why, we'd though you'd never get here, just look at you! and hug you so tight because physics can't tell you everything before they cross over into memory. And these platelets of color—the scarf, the road, the skin—speak to Goethe as if he were a plum! Imagine that, Goethe, the great German poet who needs no introduction, a plum. His violet theory of tumult says you have these things as something else, which is your usual theory approach, platelets of color rushing toward the open wound of the day to stanch it from bleeding too far into that something else. Commando-action Goethe, Wolfgang the

Goth, Wolfman, "old wild Wolf" sees it crossing his vacant shadow like an early school bell in camouflage pants. And is he scared? Hello, they say, hello-ee-lo-lo.

SINN FÉIN GORLI DROGUE

My children, said the wall and fell silent... "again" or "forever," intervals arguing their separate spastic musical theorems like gangplanks or Dutch beds, arguments plump as the side of a hay barn about to burst into flame, "my children" attaching less of everything to something, some one thing that cannot be resolved, not even "for" example, and therefore true and out of reach. Surely everything gets banked up against something somewhere like these immortal plastic shopping bags stuck in the trees, something which saves it from drifting away until you don't notice it anymore, so that the cabinet doors rattle like crazy until a bed pops out fully made, pillows fat as ravioli bouncing a couple of times on top of the covers because of their absolute perfection. Makes you want to bounce on the covers too. In your drawers. My children said the wall as if it were going deeper inside itself like a musical theorem in Boston, which appears self-evident once you see it written out, death somehow mysteriously already drifting through you. The plump Dutch silence of the sky carrying two big buckets of milk from the barn cannot get into this style of argument unless it has a bouncy rhythm to set its clogs tapping like a mechanical knitting machine. Click click click, go the needles, tapping blindly down the itchy path they weave. My children, said the wall as if these stones, this music, could speak, not about some secrets of their nature, but to us, as if we were theirs to love, and they did love us for ourselves alone.

THE LIGHTHOUSE FAMILY

child of earth

WILLIAM WORDSWORTH

It's enough to know what's coming and then not to live within the gauge with a thin coppery smile. A new jacket, for example, transforms "alot" into mechanical movements, salmony equations of expectation and independence, independence derived from expectations, not as you might want to christen them causes, not even results with bits of straw stuck in their hair, but a taste for some things which serves as a reminder that you are not just pulled along in the tide, so that this thought breaks through one of the Seven Seas in a lonely way sometimes, or maybe you feel like someone hacked into your memory and downloaded secret tapes of conversations that sound marvelously prophetic, life-like dreams remastered with you spending a night with the lighthouse family, salvers gleaming with fruits of sea-wrack and ruin, woe, and later, singing and drinking and looking for shooting stars. Is it not possible, asks the engineering genius, that someday the path may be established more directly? But the world as meditation ravels and unravels its sailors in black watch caps and bell bottoms, moves rubies around from jeweler to skin condition in a very prodigal manner. Who are you to think like a beacon piercing the ocean of night like that? And what do you get out of it? It must've been something I lost, is the reply you may use, just something I lost, OK? And no one will mention it again. And it will be transmitted to generations of evenings, buff-colored as a baseball, streaked with green light and grass stains, a piece of film with sprockets along the edge where the teeth bite in, dusted light from the projection room widening like a boat's wake in the air above the movie theater where we drown and laugh.

O JERUSALEM

Not a true Palatinate red, Caravaggio steals the body of Christ from connection with the Dublin airport, a design point for the really naked, the really helpless, who don't collect around things like this. What would you propose to do about it? Your own soul, for example, wandering in the lime-green light of the night-vision goggles the Army uses? The body of truth collapses through the arms of the helpless, a swale of nakedness where spring flowers such as Stinking Benjamin shy their little panties at your head when you take a peep: they're pollinated by turban-eyed flies, which causes the stink, as opposed to bees, which are the cleaner. Caravaggio steals the lime-green body of Christ, his hand tipped slowly into evening, betraying the novelistic whole with a kiss. Why would he vouchsafe such pash-ee-o-net things to us? How will our nakedness show it, our soul which is about the size of a linnet? The body dies and the soul most likely dies with it although each rendezvous seemed out of time, all chocolatey and nice, yet embroidered somehow into the puffy velvet sleeve of its embrace.

TÍR NA NÓG

Virgil held a blood-filled syringe and sang in perfect epic feet, *You'll never know if you don't know now*, and his words fell short of the kind of beautiful grouting work he is justly famous for, but they had an idle, menacing beauty. And I remember the fear I felt, small and leafy, as once when I was a boy, I rowed at low tide into the mouth of a storm drain at the end of Sheepshead Bay careful not to scrape against the walls and roof. The Virgin Mary held the mouth of the storm drain open for a minute while I let myself out. It was a close call because when you do things like that, the laws of nature can be repealed and the tide turn suddenly—although this has never ever happened in Brooklyn—and rush in, hurling me at my death from grandeur into one more thing floating in a world of shit. I believe this is what the syringe meant: it held my heart in its little glass-walled chamber, and you can imagine how I elected to jab it quickly into my arm.

BY NO STRETCH
OF THE IMAGINATION

This poem is coming on the right day because I have stopped writing in the sense when someone sees me on Mass. Ave. and asks, "What are you writing?" or "Are you writing anything?" they mean what are you writing connected to or, pardon the word, programmatic of a longer thought or interval of experience which is filtered through poetic gills opening and closing on the side of the writer's face? This is why a poet may not be all that good looking although within the species these gill-organs of inspiration are hardly noticed, or perhaps noticed as a really attractive feature, like those brightly colored fig-like things on some monkey bottoms. "The body of thought" is a good phrase when it is reported that right after Deng Xiaoping's death his corpse was dissected and his corneas removed, two shimmering snails popped out of their shells, so that a comrade may no longer tread this earth's salty crust in darkness, feeling with his or her feet the passage of events—so many people!—as cadence only. Now Comrade Deng-Eyes sees what before had been rumor: "like the rest of us" he thinks happily, for the first time in his life trying out this phrase as he once imagined using it, and straps to his feet the barrel staves of his former singular existence to ski away down the side of Mt. Life. Their civilization, however, is too ancient not to have recognized they were really haruspicating around in his entrails, or to put it another way, while strip-mining his natural body, they were also looking for a saga of fate or destiny, which is what that question "What are you writing?" has become: what are you discovering "for the rest of us" to use as lenses to see into or through, or maybe for the first time, at? But where the troll bridge crossing says, Hmm, this will be meaningful, the road sometimes throws its face to the ground and cries; or if I strike my forehead against the bronze-sandaled foot of the day, it is justice and love and knowledge I desire. But to be perfectly honest, I am lonely for Sheepshead Bay and my father and the boat we had. You should feel free to fill in the blanks about that statement as, metaphorically speaking, I walk around this room dressed like a gypsy violinist at Cafe Zwyzwyski, stopping at your table to whisper these lines while you talk or drink, allowing their music to become part of you, but I'm pretty certain about this: I have a very direct wish to feel on a daily basis sea spray coming over the bow and stinging my eyes, especially during the winter, and to wear bright yellow rubber pants held up by huge suspenders. A blind person's wish to see is no less real than this scene in my mind, and I feel I cannot see again without it, but where will I find the eyes to sew into my face to bring me to this boat? And how, if I don't, will I ever stop despising poetry?

JIGS AND REELS

1.

In a funny way the present is just a vanishing point which you can see through like a screen which also supports your own reflection although you may not even have been cured. Because what do I see now that I am thinking of you and you had other sons who are looking at something else? Maybe one does not need to be cured at this moment. But you cannot hold that in reserve for when you do need a cure and therefore become a screen yourself, astonished that the cause of all that gazing into the washbasin could never be connected to the blossoming freshness of the extent of things as the portion of each refrain begins as if anew next to the rhetorical question, Maybe your other sons are dead and therefore it falls to me to argue this case from the bits of images ringing your name like a collar of ice.

2.

If one looks in a mirror it is one's likeness reflected there. That is a rhetorical question which will not help if you say I am blind and therefore ignorant of the laws of fate and attraction because the outcome uses necessity. No one just as easily says "Look at this keyboard, it's impossible to make sense out of that, these must be lies!" and throws all the problems of language into the fire because the answer did not lie flat across the face of our natural expectation and desires, natural meaning anything I suppose, but not dismissive or the sense that there is no measure against which the projection of those expectations and desires should be judged. That would be crazy. Nevertheless, we could see through even that, and it would add to this feeling of clarity, like ice-skating at night and the starry crystal hissing beneath your blades as they carve out dreams of what is after all voluble.

3.

For why would I be standing here like this, pleading a case for sufficiency only, in which affliction and the placement of effects carry you away to the end of something like a brook mindlessly fidgeting with its bra strap, although the terms of this argument are never very clear and decline recognition, in the grammatical sense, so that they become the immediate language of knowledge and memory, not in any passive way, not really because of but by them, how the outcome uses necessity as you float backwards through them to the truth?

4.

Immune to all this stuff, serious, not a matter for too much judgment, all intention and pleasure at the half door! Ultimately you pick up on prodigality, thick as the mantle of fallen leaves: "What was I thinking?" raising your hand with the palm turned inward to give yourself a conk on the head; or: these are sticks for my blindness, one touch of a finger as the database swivels its hooded face to look at you, to look right through you, because the outcome uses necessity and the system is never overloaded or the reservoir drained to dangerously low levels because everyone knows it always fills up again.

PRACTICAL LULLABIES FOR JOE

this jade jar contains life

JOE TORRA

The curve of vision fails and wooden lines nailed to the floor.

Your heart is a big lump of raw red meat. At night zombies come to eat it, but they are scared away by heart-eating cranes, which also fly in to feast.

Number the things you want in order of importance starting from your age now, and an example of knowing it's true.

I think you will discover there is no cure for the zombies/ crane thing I mentioned earlier. The good news is it is rarely fatal; the bad news is the mess in the morning.

Baron Roger Von Crotchstein is a royal pain in the neck sometimes, isn't he?

For future reference: jade, the object and the word, I have never liked. The color jade is the absence of color. I pray I will never meet someone named Jade, especially if she pronounces it zsa-day.

Go to sleep, knowing the aggrieved have already chartered school-bus companies from now until the end of time, a yellow and black ribbon of certainty that stretches from the slopes of Areopagitica to America Online. Sleep, knowing they will not leave without you.

Dr. Hermann Von Languagestein is as difficult as his cousin the Baron.

Princess Zsa-Day then banished me from the kingdom, saying "That is an extremely valuable tale of connection, but they have no joy in knowing anything." For years, I planned insurrection: training with the U.S. Navy Seals in Quantico, Virginia; then, for five years, living with a family of real seals off the Oregon Coast. Seals by the way are huge pornographers: pictures of mollusks with their shells open—wide open—that sort of thing. They are also staunch believers in the First Amendment—*their* First Amendment which reads, "Death to all mollusks."

Never did I return to the kingdom of my banishment. Instead, I have chosen to live off the Oregon Coast among the pornographic but otherwise noble and kind seals. I don't give a crap about mollusks anyway. And tomorrow I receive the seals' highest honor: the Coral Wreath. Too bad I dislike coral as much as jade. I suppose I can live with it, for where on this dustproof ocean will I go next? Who will take me in? And fate is endless.

PERIPHERAL VISION

1.

Laughter, saw-toothed light, and through it all the edges of
things unseen at first, turning out to be ample in themselves,
complete, and in a sense not to be trusted, as when you look
at anything up close it is jeweled beyond belief. The seasons
therefore are another direction we have taken, a larger one and
diagonal, going on above us like immense swatches of cloth to
a patched and muddy field. You say it doesn't take much time.
But the distance is not ours, the shout at the back of things
which is falling away at such incredible speeds you hear it only
as a sigh, tracing it in the path of these too-deliberate clouds
shading across a river, plane over plane, enormous sheets of
water. But during the day it is ropes.

2.

"Then what gets canceled now?" Something sailing
marvelously, a single white ephemeron whose intemperate
dance at this exquisite moment only signals that here is
another bizarre expression we have failed to call to mind;
that perspective does not exist, least of all the kind we want
moving these dots around at night. Sounds are heard, or not.

Distance exists, but only as the tightest bridge of single white ephemera. So, it will not matter what the fates have done, disgusting things trying to rub themselves up against you. Out of these elements there is crystal: steep, goat-like steps slogging upward across selected streets. It is midtown in its most gigantic phase, and you its sweetest thief.

3.

These fragments, then, are like ice on that earliest morning when your breath comes in anticipation of something (you don't know what), but the air is so charged with connection, the sky so blue in its low curving, and the roads impassable. The day is studded with these, and your eyes are more like motes in sunlight than anything which is passing from layer to gemmed layer. There is no discourse we can hold with gorgeousness. Visions lose themselves along these spiny prisms, or we just get tired, the sails flump down around us still lashed ridiculously to the mast. But we can return, and it will not be different, only less kind. Things will uncoil towards us, original colors will revive, plinth and lintel purl.

4.

I knew it was going to work that way, and could have said so "in that look" and meant it, too. "We all have secret palaces," you said, "I used to crawl down through the moss and pearls, where the French word for little whirlpool was. The stream was so cold it made me dizzy." Like so many of the things I know, I've heard the part about the true beginnings and

44

the connections later on, the part about starry-pointed appearances in the shade, and I know this is what we mean by choice: more is hidden so we will want that too. Whatever happens could have happened. The important lessons are our own, welling up around us in the lawn chairs, and like the tide within the lawn chairs, so that we are surprised to find out where they turn up next. I say I know, but if it hadn't worked out that way, if on the other side I hadn't seen the silver line along the trees streaming into your hip, I wouldn't have known anything, all of it falling in behind me like a gulf.

FLAME COAT

1.

It takes this boy to throw so hard if you could save yourself, a flame coat to put a watch over a field or, to make itself laugh in a way we don't know, a catch in his voice as the river remembered it—in our years—later: not for him but completely: pre-canceled cells in his body turning in their homework over the internet. The search was for the leaf-covered spot that could not be wounded, where no blood showed, ever, on the troll cot.

2.

Heard stars are sweeter, a couple of ideas all swirled up like a cowlick you can't brush down, distanced in the thought of stopping: the grass all nice and sticky, a barn that looks like it could never be mistaken in anything you do with it, accommodating its timbers to change as sturdily as fate with bits of straw in your hair.

3.

The ordinary phone patch, played into the milkweed, turning your name over in my mouth. The river pushes him down for later when it'd be sister or brother to something to be: postmark on a stamp filming the day, catch in the voice as you might say forever and ever.

4.

Mottled like a turtle's shell, cracked shearling, everything at its own cause the way it wanted to be, not without specialness, but not special either, or alone: brother with brother, brother with brother and sister, sister with sister, all the way up and down the line, a team much stronger than yours, and no letting go of the moonlit axle.

5.

Attributes and qualities rustled through it, mind-reading without tongues or ripeness, not even what road the ground takes. Flame coat on the Gran Torino remembered him, put sweetness in his voice to catch him thinking about it for the river who had pushed him down that he could throw so hard, the drive-in screen like a postage stamp on the night sky.

6.

And if you could save yourself to throw so hard, the river pushes him down to remember this of him—for him, something of it, that he could change back.

LYRICAL BALLADS

Vicki said she had a child from a previous relationship, and the ocean is the Saltines of time, to find not just yourself, the single grammatical soul fluttering like a syringe above the miniature Japanese forests of scrub oak on Nantucket, certainly not clarity or truth in the cross hairs of heaven. The ocean tosses its lace panties at your feet, and we'd like to have a voice in it, our lost soul, working part-time at Congdon's Pharmacy after the divorce. The previous child absorbs changes of light on the ocean, maybe is the changes of light on the ocean, releasing them like cake for our pharmaceuticals during the intervals between sea captains returning with their stupid chanteys, receiving their traditional welcome: "Pee-yoo, is that whale piss I smell? Look out, I'm going to vomit!" Each of us is previous, a syntax of light and cake. Vicki said she'd like to be in a relationship again, the Japanese art of miniaturization applied to a nice new pair of panties shining white against her tanned legs. And though the soul as we know it is lost, except as a tasty Saltine like a mouthful of miniature ocean, out of its blubbery absence there is this love.

SECENT IMAGE

1.

Even a faucet is greater, and the bright wrist asserts neither expectation nor ignorance, this incredible radiant traction we have. Won't you ever learn, each loss promoted on the branch of days, except now everything stands for everything else without recognition or fear or truth, plush and dark, filled with friends and stars clinking in your summer glass, music of confidence and despair? Or some mark you could lean against or cross with silage, knowing what is exacted, at least until description licks its finger and draws the outline of a boat on your lips. How will I be known? Nothing exceeds description which is bigger than necessity, a patchwork quilt that shows how we live in the dative case. One types, "There are no silhouettes, canvas bass notes ascend the mirrored disc, not as cause or continuation, but how one winter I took my gloves off eager to chop ice out of a boat cover," and that this is all you ever wanted: to reclaim the parts of language and death that belong to you.

2.

But not for what they cannot offer to be known, a funny kind of absence of a refrain that nothing will ever be like this again. So many had been like description, a language of dying that is not about loss, "*secent* image" written with dignity, comprehension, error. A language of dying to implore this image: give me nothing back; this is for you; this is how I see you, I could trace you forever. So they stand in for what is absent. You couldn't make them into anything else, and what they are is a set of tools for perception and leave-taking, something temporary for something permanent, which though not yet known is not unknown in terms we're now familiar with. So many had been like description. Not a photograph, at least not a photograph as you might hear it discussed on the T, at the Charles Street/Massachusetts General Hospital station, before the train arches its neck into the tunnel's black water again.

3.

Memory isn't paginal: pointing to the mantle of falling leaves, it offers its critique of pure reason as being out of it, then rustles through the database as a portion of fate or recognition so that all entries smell faintly of tannin, braiding (or unbraiding) invisible cords of expectation and desire lashed to your wrist, shining like a kiss—not as knowledge or dimension, but that nothing can be greater than any image of our loss, and everything will have to catch up with that: knowledge as only description, a grammar of vanishing points like the slender dark cone of your voice so that the plane of surfaces doesn't just dissolve (we begin with that premise) or slant so fully in its descent that we walk between them, or disappear behind them or into them, reflected against these surfaces like graffiti, like leaves banked up against a wall.

4.

No, the reality of that never completes itself in us, a grammar that lets you see not what isn't there (we begin with that premise too) but that it isn't there is a recognition forever (although that never completes itself in us either). That's what memory is, isn't it? The other side of the photograph brought forward as the real subject, how we drift in a sort of sideways scallop motion through the page, piling up instances of these unknown conditions, or reflected by them in a kind of virtual presence. That it isn't there in the sense that each object describes what it just missed, so that it's funny how you see through them, yet delight in them because they are shed off like that.

5.

So, the necessary conditions are unknown. On a wall someone writes *shadow* or *logic*, or *This arrogance will be your undoing Mister Demonicus,* and sees right through it. Maybe not to anything, but that after all was where we started a minute ago. Memory then is just this sort of unspecific recognition that we're not going to see anything anyway, and that all we do is process (wordprocess, if you like) descriptions of what we feel is missing. It's like you were disappearing sometimes. So, these slant through the plane of the picture like a triangle, one leg declining over the other, completed by leaves banked up on the other side of the photograph. *Dear Angle*. One types "Happiness and other forms of terror," or "Loss, a new coin in your pocket," and "Don't be afraid, I went in there and I came out again," heroic and kind, human too for what it cannot offer to be known in someone else's case, and ultimately how separated we are although in the early dark once the clocks have been turned back it's not the individual windows but the whole block lit up like an airplane turning out of the page of the sky, "Shudder in one leg of the journey."

6.

Dear Angle, There are no silhouettes, falling out of the page of the sky, as if someone turned the photograph over to see what was written on the other side. This wall is made up of shadows and each one drifts sideways through the page of the day in a sort of scallop motion like a falling leaf, not as cause or continuation but how so many had been like description of some other object which they reflected or maybe sketched the outline of. But no, not what wasn't there, but there only after you saw it, because you saw it, which is important to remember, this portion of fate or recognition which you think is in there, how they drift down out of the day, and you feel you are looking through them to someone else, not really at them. Nevertheless, they should be pressed to your lips as they used to say because they're not hiding anything, nor are they translations appropriating something that doesn't belong to them and, therefore, because they are dying, these things we have which seem to be about so many other things.

the BOSTON TRILOGY

(THREE PROSE POEM NOVELS)

Tell on You (2003)

Kevin White (2007)

Bosston (2008)

*I had several more lives to live and could not spare any
more time for that one.*

WALDEN, OR, LIFE IN THE WOODS
HENRY DAVID THOREAU

from TELL ON YOU

(2003)

FOR A COWPER SNOW GLOBE

Like shooting turkeys in a barrel, said the road, who didn't
know a lick of vernacular, or had become it, a field filling
with loosestrife. Expectation outweighs desire for most of a
life. Here is the body filled with fluids, lifegiving and baneful,
draped in high-gloss advertisements for bra and panties, all
shiny and clean from chemicals like a pharmaceutical, or the
more remanded form of men's drawers and T-shirts made
from natural cotton fibers, treated and bleached, threading
your eyes and mind to the pages of the Sunday *New York
Times Magazine*; or expectation wired to its own weight in
knowledge and memory, black-and-white ads for lingerie in
The Boston Globe.

The plasma of things doesn't know me very well, does it?
Blank, gray squibs of sky seep through the dutchments of my
body—"sky" or "time" or time's sky or its story that includes
me now and then, as always. Thank God it doesn't know its
own strength or I'd be crushed under the stony ground after
it pulled out all my hair in clumps and let me cast no shadow
anymore, motioning with one arm to cross the street while
with the other arm a crossing guard makes a line of cars wait
for me.

Here's what we mean by life: all the rules are rescinded except the ones that keep things standing, and it's bigger and whip-like, uncoiling with a snap that flicks the quivering cigarette out of the lovely actress's mouth so she can go back to licking and being licked. Sometimes it just slides in and out like a mink through the boards at the base of a barn wet with snow melt. Here's what we mean by life: I want to be the street. Because some things are immortal in keeping with the personal, it offers each one more access to the rest. It tells each beading mystery with chalky fingers.

If it's all the same to you, I might "shed" some tears, which is the language for Gore-Tex apparel whose porous, miraculous weaving sheds rain and snow while letting your own natural moisture, your sweating armpits and back, your crotch and buttocks, return their prayerful wetness to the environment which gave them life and which we should protect at all costs: where else can we turn, foretold or ordained or probable, given the laws, the carbon-fiber length and duration, the humid, diffuse ichor?

The soul is a carved wood napkin ring in the center of your chest. There is a complex system or network, a web of tubing designed to support the body around it. The soul is separated from capillary action, which is a theorem of the body smartly agreed to by the fathers of the church, whose portraits rest above a cloud-filled, absent base. The ring is pitted and worn from toxins which gravitate toward all living things like revenuers to moonshine in a backwoods still. There is a needle-thin sliver of soap about to evaporate at the edge of the bathroom drain which is your soul.

Do you see the running jump? I think we can make it. I think we can make it through the night, goes the lymph gland under my arm. I mean, this is a lyric of a popular song from the 80's, minus the gland. I think we can take the cusp and this is February. I think there is a panic in my tubing. The sun presents its fission of heaven, the vibration of nice things and the vibration of bad things interact on earth giving us a taste for a vibrating subset of these things. The wavy lime-colored lines on a hospital monitor where *We perish'd, each alone* could be engraved—here, let me give it a good shake like a snow globe and watch the shimmering green and radiant flakes float down.

LADY

Through misery and pain, sang the mirror, and the blossoming freshness of the extent of things, the way things are, and nature, which includes you too, and wants to hold in your hands that spiky little brush you lengthen your eyelashes with, the powdery chalks you draw across your cheek, and nibble through the spectra of—and here the mirror paused, then resumed—crayons the consistency of Philadelphia Cream Cheese that you stroke your lips with: you have allowed nature to imagine these things too, you have let her understand what her endless wanderings were for: look how she wants to color your hair, sang the mirror when you were in the shower.

But it's hard laughing up the hanging sleeve of the extent of things pointing past you—this time—to the person in the seat behind you, Yes, you ma'am, would you mind coming up on stage, never to be seen again through the encouraging, relieved applause. You feel like Joey Bishop. His face was the grave of the joke he was about to tell, cheerless as an approach to the Van Wyck Expressway, a blankness I think older Jews in Brighton Beach "got" but moved past to Buddy Hackett and Shecky Green, even Norm Crosby. They had "an act" that could at least reach into the straw-filled wind and pull down a bolus of veal or chicken to chew on through the first show of the stripping, mob-owned night.

One can drift in ignorance with a kind of rebar sturdiness, yet a lightness and a lyricism—at least for a while. You have to be quick when you're young and ignorant. So it was not surprising that one took to boxing as one might, in a different setting, take to dance or poetry, or, in this setting, how some took to heroin, which was just beginning to come into this Brooklyn Irish neighborhood like a dog hunting on the scent of a wounded animal, in this case families already mortally wounded by alcohol. These were ways—boxing, drinking, heroin—to strip down and be seen and wondered at and feared, and to effect some sort of end by having to struggle in front of others attending to the only spectacle that is ever worth watching, one's mindless fight against being alive.

We were prepositions hanging on, modifying, slightly, the larger sentence. Engraved on a plaque in front of the church near the gym were the psalmist's words: "God is in the midst of the city," and I figured it meant, here in this church, the way "Liquors" showed where you bought Schaefer beer or "Drugs" on Doc's meant here is where you got prescriptions filled. "Be still, and know that I am God," a knowledge we get by listening to the psalmist tell the desolation visited upon his enemies. But that only raised the question, what was the need for wasting a bunch of nobodies in a marginal part of the city which belonged more to the ocean than to the city streets which we walked barefoot on in summer and in winter waited for a car to stop at the light so we could squat down behind it and grab its rear bumper and let it pull us in our Thom McAnn's sliding through the snow when the light changed? Whose enemies were we except our own?

The Lady is not able, like the boat he shipped out on, to connive with strangeness and nature. He cannot return successfully. He cannot work as a greeter in Vegas, someone a little bit larger than life—a boxer and a merchant marine—to make you feel special when you walk in. He has no stories to tell of sailing back from Africa. No one feels saltiness in his handshake. The ocean does not bell out to the wheelhouse stars, the desert shrinks to the canvas inside the ring.

But seriously, as the biblical Jewish comic "I see before me" might say—a blend of Rickles and Lewis, Norm Crosby, Joey Bishop and Isaiah, none of them ever really that far from the dog-tongue waves of Brighton Beach that just want to lick your longed-for face—*Seriously, I kid with the spilkes in the gnechtigazoid, with the love and the telling and pretty l-a-a-d-y!* And the desert sands, transfixed by the immutable sun, enjoyed a drink on the house in the old days' young nights, its legs dusted with stars showering down the cool Sahara dunes.

CHILDREN IT WANTS BACK MAYBE

Growing up around boats and the junk they'd leave when we hauled them out of the water—it's funny how even when I felt trapped by what I had been given as my portion of the ripening extent of things, those invisible gills we have for knowing more than what we see filtered out a lot of the toxins that will kill me, a mussel opening its shiny black visor out of Caravaggio for the filthy water to come in and feed.

You knew and you didn't know, same difference. You were seeing things. Things the ocean puked up. Things it let you have after it was done playing with them. Things of its own, ripped from its breast. Things it steered right into your hands. Things before the body and after the body. Things never recorded or paid off the books. Things reaching into the blackboard night with chalky fingers. Things you knew by heart.

And the ripening extent of things falling in the world and the waves that drown and bank them up against jetties or piers or buoys fitted with bells that welcome as they ward away: things we know, or at least know about, things you know yourself when you have to go, treading water as the pee streams out from between your legs and you think it'll go on forever and someone will figure out what you're doing motionless in the different density of the liquor around your thighs, dropping your hands to flap the crotch of your swimsuit a couple of times to get it all out before you swim into a cleaner current of the stupid immortal ocean.

You know yourself a lot less than washing a Hanes cotton T-shirt. The curved lapstrake hull bells out a path through the ocean's unthought-of usernames, tipped darkly in a following sea down the impassable mouth of a wave, wheels in a block of wood the size of a dog's head pulling ropes and rusted chains thick as lamentation.

The struggle around boats is against the natural tendency of things to be open to other things, to leak or let pass through, or not be able to inhibit transit, or perhaps wanting to be the medium of some other expression of will or desire or love, the hooded blue wave curling over a face turned to the side in neither disbelief or wonder or fear or acceptance. To grow up around boats is to be with what they spread at your feet, swelling with what they have become in their conniving with strangeness and nature: the struggle with waves coming at you like a music video changing expression and bodies with biblical disregard for narrative, a line of young arms at spring training throwing for the media. Gods rise to the surface, and then above it; slaves and their children with sores around their mouths sink below the surface which is chucking at their chins, knocking off their paper crowns rimmed with candles like a birthday cake, sipping at their runny noses in the exchange of fluids an ocean lives for, hulling out the body like a bell.

What it spreads at your feet with a wave of its hand or lets drip darkly down its implacable iron face rusted with circulation: children it wants back maybe, children it made for lesser but more durable things.

AND THE RIPENING EXTENT OF THINGS FALLING IN THE WORLD

she looked with quaint affection at the diminutive body
which she had so often adorned

JAMES JOYCE, "CLAY"

Nothing outweighs description which is bigger than necessity, a language of expectation falling back on the new-made bed after a shower, inhaling the smell of fresh linens, sinking into the pillow to just the right depth, rubbing her bare arms over the sheets a couple of times to feel the perfection of a thing doing what exactly it was meant to do. The ripening extent of things falling in the world. And later, as evening returns with its soft *so,* not as accusation or reproof, but really an honest question, and human—do you know what you have got yourself into? what has gone on? too much time, or too little time?

Forgiveness lashed to the body in its nakedness, wanting its stories about the imperishability that dies and will not go away, the maw's shell waiting on the strangely bleached sand, and expectation and desire ripening the extent of things: a sense of justice, a sense of how the world *should* work; or maybe just a taste for things prompt and tricky, a morality rigorous and nonchalant and quick as us: *there's no denying it* as the phrase goes, triumphant or resigned, body naked as a hinge, bending over the wet tongue of the story for its truth to be licked. Language of recognition and desire. Prophecy, a body thing. How will I know you, hooded face turned to the side in neither disbelief or wonder or fear or acceptance? This is what I do. This is how I do it. Will I be open to you, to let pass through me or not be able to inhibit transit or perhaps wanting to be the medium of, to want you more than I can represent it: remanded forms that also are the case, and the impassable mouth of the wave?

Leave me a shell, chalk it up to the characters, the plot, the scenery, even the audience who plays along: the way things are, consequent and necessary, never and always sufficient, pilings driven into the marly bottom to carry into all that is impassable, never to be seen again through the encouraging waves slapping up their sides like applause. Where else can I turn? And the ripening extent of things falling in the world, and waves that drown and bank them up against jetties or piers or buoys fitted with bells that welcome as they ward away, reaching into the blackboard night with chalky fingers to scrawl all the things I know by heart, things you know yourself before we have to go. That evening at Plum Beach, those big summer nights still ahead of us, and the beach so empty and abundant. "Let's go for a swim." Standing a few feet apart to strip down to our underwear, bra and panties that looked like a bikini, Jockey shorts that no-way looked like a Speedo, and walking out of the waves like a wash coming out of the machine.

from KEVIN WHITE

(2007)

KEVIN AND JOHN

[John Wieners had two visions of the Virgin Mary, the poet Jim Dunn said after Wieners' funeral Mass in Milton, Massachusetts. Dunn used to visit Wieners at his Joy Street apartment in Boston, sometimes followed by lunch at Burger King. When asked if Mary spoke to him during her first visitation, Wieners replied she was just learning English. Ten years later, after his second vision, he said she had put on a few pounds. Kevin White was mayor of Boston from 1968 to 1984.]

I saw Kevin White's mind disappearing into heaven as he bent down to pick up a tea bag John Wieners left on I-93 Southbound to remind oncoming traffic and the Big Dig that we have been set to—Boston, a mound of curly, tight shiny law in the mind of Kevin our charge—and holding it like a ribbon to give a pretty girl, he placed it on his tongue and spoke to the Virgin Mary his language of tannin.

Every city looks the same on a day like this, wrote the iron window grate in the broad-nibbed hand of an original signer or natural philosopher of the ways of us in buckled shoes and silk hose, stubby sleeves with big split cuffs, and the end in which ev-uh-ree-thing is to be seen, muddy fog dripping from a grate in its carapace of black enamel rustproofing and idle sea crest.

Virgil charges his cares at Boston Latin to be worthy of Kevin and John: this, even this for the merit of things, not as cause or effect, but gathered in the folds of revelation, the memenissean moment raveling and unraveling the Libya of its dunes.

HÖLDERLIN IN BOSTON

the breakfast table is seemingly instant

JOE TORRA

Laws drown under the wide-planked sky's plump hull, or the No. 86 to Cleveland Circle slashes its action-figure kanji over Wheelwright's idea of bridges from the Netherlands, each a windmill blade dreaming on the hills of heaven, to bear in mind a thin-gauged copper thought that will go astray because it is not a revelation or a prophecy. And because they long to reach beyond bounds, the bus, the bridge, the thought are tested on earth with symmetry and example. Things ripen. Fire rhymes with silver, and what will you do, likening ornamental scrolls to waves churning across the loss of eternity, mice that scratch as greedily at the poison you put out as at your crumbs? Water is a TV. Violets would watch TV if they could, like children, and turn to heaven with a question unfulfilled. Some things are infusions, some radiation. The water table chews across generations to slip houses in the South End. Hilly Somerville funnels rainwater under basement floorboards, a majestic train of starry mold in its wake. Balance is unattainable except by those for whom loyalty is impossible.

Sentences of dirt and light, violet-eyed children turn their faces toward a heavenly world above water. On their shoulders prophecy and measure carry them away to the end of something, and earth is fulfilled in their wandering. They have no home, but born into dreams of life, cling to the moonlit axle churning through them. Daylight affirms everything to the point of derision and waves of description lap us out to sea.

The breakfast table above your knees would live like a bridge in the sun, a slender form, deaf to ripening comparisons but with enough weight of example to be symmetrical and instant. To walk contained, returned to a distance measured in bread crumbs, is earth's violet law which children use to color the face of heaven's action figures. "St. Catherine died when she fell out of a cherry tree," said Fanny Howe's grandson. Trued to their axles of rain and falling snow, the bread, the cherry tree, the violet saint—will we ever get through them like a thick book?

NATURAL LAW

To those of born divine

JOHN WIENERS

Coppered with fallen leaves, or slashed by an industrial-strength carp jumping with Oriental disdain for background, the Charles River takes its iron color from vegetation steeping in it like a tea bag, not from PCBs or pollution, a mottled latex condom in slow drift on the river's dream of heaven. It is a natural state of being for the Charles River, and we want to live as naturalized citizens in this ripening state, *Gleich Krystallen in der Wüste wachsend*, "Like crystals growing in the waste," with balance and simplicity, abundance in remove from thought and language, all proudly baseball-stitched into the truth.

All "uninvoluntarily" the State House dome floats golden as a child's Burger King crown above houses built on pilings driven into Back Bay's Flemish mound like birthday candles into a moist cake, a loud flailing in answer to dreams of permanence, children amiss in the arraignment of wishes.

Born unspared the revelation of contingency as memory rising of its own eagerness to what it already knows, not as fate or symmetry or example, but expectation, desire—what else should I address as Mary?

This requisite conflagration: enough has been torn from screens to approach that, even before new curtains are drawn in droves, a sweetness of cake in mouths open blind, haul and winnow of late-night TV, clapped chalk sugared through midnight classrooms.

Municipal life, an organ of want beyond bounds, floats the sunflower dome of the Commonwealth of Massachusetts State Capitol Building, its face turned to a world above water. John Wieners' body, papered like a wasp's nest, waves a sunflower in front of Kevin's eyes, and because of its brilliance, and John's big stomach, Kevin cannot look around it for his skyline, its source of gold a remonstrance to him. John offers its seedy face to Kevin, and puts it on his head for a crown; then, clutching him like a mother, in her transparent hand a child's terry-cloth Cardinal's robe, starry raiment wet with tears, she holds sleeping Kevin on her lap in front of the Hancock Tower's giant flat-screen TV, Red Sox ahead, and Pedro, his pitch count high, waving Little off.

The day starts and stops, a change takes place, and stars come out in their underwear, countermured with diamond. It's stupid and marvelous, like a play written by a horse: hoof mark, hoof mark, straw—don't step in Act Two. Ripeness is all we get? That doesn't sound right: you love it, the it you see and the it you know is in there. And you want it to love you back with all the deliciousness and sorrow of a natural law that has no words for its corollaries and terms shadowed on the hillside, washed in the apples.

NOMAR

Law in the mind of Kevin our charge is fresh from his haircut. She offers to know unconditional terms in pinwheels and dots of razor burn drying on his neck. The symmetry and example of a French-blue shirt to Kevin's deep-set eyes even the garden statue of Mary, her arms open wide, palms out, cannot contest in sadness and confusion over white fish-tank pebbles strewn at her feet.

Joseph Abboud went to UMass Boston says the commercial to wash off Billy Bulger's DNA and put on a clean shirt fresh from the clothesline where it revels in its bodilessness, free of chest and armpits chalked with deodorant, deeper than appearance, deeper than lungs and heart the size of a summer lemon. It smells clean and fresh, and Kevin's health aid takes it from the bureau and shakes it out with a smart snap like a jib catching a gust of wind off Fort Point Channel. He draws it over the mayor's left arm, across his back and over the right arm; he stands in front of him and angles buttons through their little slits, starting with one below his collar, and finishing with one above his crotch, then quickly runs the flat of his hand bladewise across and down the small of the mayor's back to tuck in the shirttail, and around the front of his waistband to press into Kevin's lap the dignity and hem of a Joseph Abboud shirt.

William Corbett saw Nomar Garciaparra in Charlie's Sandwich Shop on Columbus Avenue in Boston after the Red Sox lost to the Yankees in Game 7 of the 2003 American League Championship Series, hugged him in silence, turned and left. "The body is a kind of soul," he wrote in fealty to things, the ocean off Cape Cod which cakes your lips with delicious New England salt water filtered through mussels gathered in buckets and steamed with white wine and garlic to pry open their shiny black visors out of Caravaggio; or a world as blue and green as it can be, lit in God's own sunshine by orange daylilies, zinnias and sunflowers: on the table fried eggplant with a brandywine heirloom tomato sauce, small onions fried with a coating of flour, milk, pecorino Romano cheese and Italian parsley; roasted corn salad with lime, maple syrup and bacon; a grilled marinated loin of pork, and later, deep-dish blueberry tart. In rainy Somerville, private morning writing time closes with a letter: "I'll be seeing you before we know it as time passes like water. Got to go now, the girls are stirring and I've got to get them breakfast. Leftover pasta with sauce for Julia, taquitos for Celeste. Love, Joe."

The body to uncarry itself and be seen for what Nomar did at shortstop, evening sky above Fenway scuffed by planes taking off from Logan, off balance, diving to the right, one hop off the infield grass, a soft green stain where the ball's red stitching cinches in like the waist of Sargent's *Madame X*.

And the end in which ev-uh-ree-thing is to be seen? Allston—Brighton—after thirty years of self-imposed exile in Boston you are still my indistinguishable Sacco and Vanzetti in Ben Shahn's portrait of two men with the hollow stare of all those infants on Mary's lap in Renaissance paintings leaning in and away to the nursing home where my mother at 90, unable to feed herself, unable to wash the products of her body from her body says, "I wish I had more time." Time not measured in time: waving away a priest because everyone in Boston had money and went to the Harvard of President Lowell who could find no bias against Sacco and Vanzetti, no "*onderstanding* of man as now we do by accident," as Vanzetti wrote. More time to see Jennie and the girls, more time for repeats of *Everybody Loves Raymond,* Saturday afternoon golf tournaments because she didn't need the sound on to look at tanned and marvelous young men walking the earth beneath her feet.

The body to uncarry itself and be seen, not as image or memory on rails of character like the Green Line out to Brookline and Kitty Dukakis, which is Greek for *All fate is local, Michael,* all love, all distinction and honor and joy, all loss, all abundance, all body, all soul. *Let the Irish take it, mo cushla,* Kitty sang from the end of Anthony's Pier 4 and pierced her cheek with a fish bone glimmering in a dumpster before she jumped into Boston harbor. *Catch me, mo cushla, catch your little silver trout.*

THE BIG DIG

The contractor who says over his shoulder, "This will last longer than you," and turns away happy with this address to his skill: is that what I want to hear? A shed where I'll store what I affectionately call my shit—store, or as we say, "stow it away" as if this stuff I won't use but can't throw out is moored there, waiting on the outgoing tide—this will outlast me? What do I want to outlive me? Family of course, and any savings and assets they can use. Friends, I suppose, but I always imagine we'll begin to drop off around the same time, in super-old age, movie style: "A telegram for you, Senator Barrett," says the wide-hipped Irish nurse, watch pinned to her ample, starched bosom as she hands me an envelope. I look up from my wicker wheelchair. Nurse folds her dove-winged arms in silence as camera tracks in for close-up of my eyes reading telegram. Conflicting emotions on dramatically wrinkled face under chalky grey wig. Quick cut to hands dropping telegram on lap covered with tweed shawl. Camera pulls back until, framed by tasteful lifetime clutter in upstairs Commonwealth Avenue sick room, Barrett delivers his line: "Dickie Bonesworth is gone... dear Dickie... old Bonesy." Music. Fade out.

Speaking of my dear dickie, it makes no sense that fingernails and hair grow after I'm put in the clay—proof enough to refute intelligent design in favor of a patchwork quilt to wander in ransom with the FBI. One last erect nipple on the cold slab, a sunflower of unspecific, vegetable lust lifting its seedy head above my tea bags during Gross Anatomy class tucked away behind Huntington Avenue's green smear, my body's Dutch door flung open to every monger of the street. I want a Viking funeral to anneal these guts with autumn pumpkin and apple peel flames, a dumpster floating up the Charles River from MIT, under the BU bridge, past the Weeks footbridge and Wheelwright's ode in brick to the windmill blade of Civil War, symmetry and example dreaming of heaven before the Nike brand swoosh of riverbank in Allston/Brighton.

In reflection the Hancock Tower's pornographic glass skin purifies the pumpkin clay roof of Trinity Church for its hajj across Boston's postage-stamp size Celtic fields where St. Catherine sits in a tree eating cherries with Fanny Howe. There are two worlds, says Fanny to the startled birds, their beaks blood red with cherry juice; collateral worlds, she continues as the birds fly off, and to posit truth in one is to beg the question in the other. Fanny climbs out of the tree, down the backstairs of a Roxbury triple-decker where Kevin White, his arms outstretched to St. Catherine, her robe spread around her like an enormous cherry pie, makes machine gun noises with his mouth.

Boston, I wanted to build a road underground where it belongs to souls of the departed, a living road, biology over biography, language over history, laws raveled from the sleeve of description. Boston, I wanted the girls in Harvard Square who wore their hair down and no make-up. I wanted to learn Irish in Quincy House. Kevin, I wanted the city I thought you saw rising in my mind. Kevin, I wanted to get on the city.

FLIGHT INTO EGYPT

I saw former Red Sox pitcher Bill "The Spaceman" Lee take something from a dumpster in front of the Corbett house. "Watch it!" said Lee, "dreams are not hard science like colonoscopy and laser hair removal—dreams don't even know your name, Mr. Wally Cox, and therefore they come to you but could just as easily visit someone else when all you wanted was to have your head patted like a child. And I am Bill Lee, making a voodoo doll of Carl Yazstremski whose dream came to me by mistake and said Yaz was living in the Corbett house, upstairs under the eaves." "Is Bill moving?" I asked, "What's he need a dumpster for, anyway?" "Ask him yourself, here he comes," shouted Bill Lee as he ran down Columbus Avenue, sideways like a crab. "Bill, I don't understand, what is this all about?" "Dreams," snarled Corbett, "Who the hell is Bill Lee to talk about dreams!" And we walked into his study which was filled with life-size voodoo dolls of Bill Lee, each wearing a different set of legs: deer legs, grasshopper legs, rat's feet, and still twitching in the corner, a doll with legs of a blue-claw crab taken from the Gowanus Canal when Bill was visiting Brooklyn where the crab population, long crushed under the weight of pollution, now floats and copulates in the currents around Brooklyn like a blue halo. "Dreams know your name,

Ed Cullen Bryant, like a real estate agent knows a price. Through my black art I torment Bill Lee with more sets of legs climbing up on him than some of the poor souls who once worked as prostitutes on Columbus Avenue. But now Boston has these dumpsters where our true past, which is unclaimed dreams, gets shoveled out each morning!" And Bill kicked the side of the dumpster so hard some trash spilled out revealing a child's Burger King paper crown from a lost day in the lost life of the nameless real, its gold paper glistening in the sun. Just then the soul of John Wieners stood beside us and when he picked up the Burger King crown and set it on his courtly brow, you could see that it wasn't paper at all, but the live body of a blue-claw crab, its shell delicately balancing on top of John's bald spot, its legs in the air like a Boston prostitute, and in each of its needley pincers a birthday candle glowing in the blue smoke of the Virgin Mary's cigarette.

from BOSSTON

(2008)

3 BODIES UNEARTHED IN DORCHESTER
BULGER CONFIDANT IS SAID TO GIVE TIP

Digging through the night shielded from biting cold, authorities early yesterday unearthed the remains of two men and a woman after being tipped off to the Dorchester burial spot by a top lieutenant to fugitive South Boston crime boss James "Whitey" Bulger.

While authorities have yet to identify the victims believed to have been killed by Bulger and his longtime cohort, Stephen ("The Rifleman") Flemmi, sources said Bulger confidant Kevin Weeks claims Arthur "Bucky" Barrett, John McIntyre, and Deborah Hussey were among the victims…

THE BOSTON GLOBE, JANUARY 15, 2000

GREEN MONSTER

This young crop knows it. Sometimes I think I could stay here forever. Then I remember what all the fuss is about. State Police labs have data to prove it. So, I spend lunch breaks on the hill taking blood samples from the soil. It will be hard to confide in anyone anymore.

L. L. Bean catalogs drifting down out of a Maine sky promising renewed life on this earth in press-free slacks and all-day comfort in shoes with advanced walking-platform construction: the sky-blue mailman's uniform as he stuffs them in the mailbox, stacks of catalogs raked in a corner of the sofa, sliding off, red and orange and yellow pages as I walk across the room.

She rescues the investigation simply by showing up: cloudy bra-straps on bronzed shoulders, fragments we learn this from. No one collected such things anymore. Lists, sure, but people who made them came from far away, and we wanted a local in the back row with a fresh haircut straight from his best friend's wedding with the bride on his arm.

A field buries the ones it began. You'd think the sky would rub the field's broad back. Yes, that's exactly what you'd think. A field stammers and falls, a Gore-Tex sky bays out saltily over Boston harbor. And they enjoyed success and levity in the mock-up stage, a roar that came from behind the scoreboard, dense and pulpy, illegible as rebar.

The soul in its witness protection program, invisible as the period at the end of this sentence.

ALL SOULS'

Boston's dead simply will not stay buried.

Ralph Waldo "The Rifleman" Emerson and Deborah Hussey Thoreau, their Platonic dream of winter sunlight reflected off the sunflower dome of the Commonwealth of Massachusetts State Capitol Building, its pilings driven into Back Bay's Flemish mound "like birthday candles into a moist cake."

A loud flailing in answer to dreams of permanence, the Big Dig uncarried by a road underground where it belongs to souls of the departed, a road in Greek, and the Institute of Contemporary Anthony's Pier 4.

A road underground with all the dutchments of the body, foretold or ordained or probable, its carbon-fiber laws of length and duration, its human diffuse ichor.

Deborah Hussey Thoreau had several more lives to live and could not spare any more time for one where the damned howled away their hearts in a useless transcendent mound off I-93.

Whitey Butler Yeats held it tight, a thought that, in it wound, he could run like Boris Karloff in *The Mummy,* run in the world's despite: "The mind is weak, and I can shrink to the size of a period at the end of this sentence, and in it need no other thing." He was a ghost-lover all right, and grew more arrogant being a ghost.

JOHN WIENERS AT FILENE'S

"Seen or encountered in Boston," wrote John Wieners in his notebook. Real or desired, a vision: Barbara Stanwyck, who had wardrobe show her stomach but asked them to cover the rest of her body, which she said was flawed. Can you hear her saying *flawed* in a Brooklyn accent? Description wants to cup your face in its hands, cradle a telephone in the crook of its transparent arm, whispering, "It's impossible to know," and "We all stand revealed." Barbara Stanwyck had wardrobe describe her body according to her body's logic: "Give a girl a break, will ya? Yeah, like that. Aw, you're a peach!" And description wants to know the impossible too, set it down for the record, a silver ribbon studded with rhinestones. If you're lucky, you hear someone mean it in terms of a clarity of feeling: "I'd do anything for you"—not totally "out there" or anything too deported from the laity of believers and the truths they take by the hand where a diamond cutout over the midriff shows Barbara Stanwyck's stomach. "Why now?" it goes in the dark, "Why, when everything was just beginning to change, my life on track again?" To cradle her body with clarity and deportment is all she was asking in her crooked accent, embracing wardrobe like a doll, a living doll.

MASS TRANSIT

Necessity gave the cold, cold hand a glove

MOONDOGGIE, IN *GIDGET*

A few. Now five. Now all these kids skating on the Charles River, our first hard freeze, some with hockey sticks sweeping an invisible puck. The reason the Dutch were so happy and prosperous was the frozen canals they skated on is a thought they are not aware of having; it is a thought the Charles River is having about them, including them in Wheelwright's dream of bridges from the Netherlands, each a windmill blade turning to a world above water with a question unfulfilled.

The body pleading its case for insufficiency: balance unattainable except by those for whom loyalty is impossible; how it offers to reach into the cone-shaped silence of a river like a child reaching for a shiny stone.

We are tempted here on earth by symmetry and example to reach beyond bounds in our wooden shoes. On their shoulders, prophecy and measure, like two big buckets of milk, sweep skaters away to the end of something fidgeting with its bra strap. They decline as grammar declines an immediate language of expectation and memory, how the outcome only used necessity as we float backwards through the truth.

Wheelwright's ode in Dutch to the American Civil War: *To A Father By A Son,* unironic as the No. 66 bus over the Larz Anderson bridge to Brookline and Michael Dukakis who must've thought he could do material for Whitey "The Mummy" Yeats and the South Boston Rat Pack at the St. Patrick's Day breakfast, his face the grave of the joke he was about to tell, a regular Joey Bishop.

from DOWN NEW
UTRECHT AVENUE

(2011)

WILLIAM WORDSWORTH, OR CURRENT RESIDENT

The light changes, and we pull back from the edge of the curb with a ruffle of people and colors in clothes like the hem of Shirley MacLaine's skirt in *Irma la Douce*. This is no piano song in front of winter birches. We stop, and the lane of traffic purges its stomach: *th-p-p-p,* cars with 0% financing; *th-p-p-p-p,* more cars with rates so low they're giving them away. This is not, quote, all who stop will one day stop, unquote, because it's snowing and the curb is the street's panty line. We're not stopped, we're not really waiting: it's like watching commercials on the late-night movie channel, where my soul, which is a kind of body, is trying out a mattress, is coloring its hair.

ANNIVERSARY YEARS

for Michael and Isabel

These are the kind of years we don't mind adding on because they also add up in a sweet way, like pitchforks full of hay until you have a haystack big enough to feed a herd of cows or set on fire as a signal in the night sky—the haystack, not the cows: setting cows on fire is unkind and illegal and an image I will not let into this poem, not even as a signal in the night sky for sailors in danger off the coast. Goodbye, cows on fire—and don't bump into anything flammable on your way out the door as you amble to the Charles River where you can douse those flames which are only imaginary so you're not really getting burned: I wouldn't do that to you although hot milk for cocoa is yummy, so if you could squeeze off a quart before you go... No, you'd better leave, lighting the way as you shamble into Porter Square, carrying milk and flames through snow falling on all those stupid shoppers at Star Market who don't realize how many sailors' lives are hanging on your every move.

TITLE BOUT

(titles for poems that cannot be written)

1.

Tears streaming down the forgotten names of St. Paul's horse, and children countless as air racing up and down these frozen canals, their skates a kind of Dutch horseshoe whose blades are sleek Alcaics, whose steely picks point away from the fallen Saul, his horse's leg bent like a shield for our eyes against the glare of Caravaggio's movie spot in an embrace of faith forming the lower arc of an oval intersecting the crossed arms of Jesus and the horse's head, trunk, and hind leg—forgotten horses whom the Bible does not sanctify with a name, unlike heroic literature which seems to take no notice of differences between immediate, inciting circumstances as distinguished from fundamental causes, or in Whitehead's phrase "the coincidence of eternal objects forming a specific point-event" such as a horse

2.

These oblique kanji slashing spider after spider, eternity unscrolling in the lobby of the Boston Mandarin Oriental Hotel financed by fugitive David K. Drumm, CEO of the Anglo-Irish Bank in Dublin whose euros are the pastel color of Gabriel's Annunciation robes "out of reach of police" on Cape Cod

3.

Memory as "prior to all knowledge," a kind of inner boxer "who is his own work and cannot decide what he wills and remains essentially the same to the very end" (Schopenhauer) because *velle non discitur*, willing cannot be taught (Seneca)

4.

The strength of a situation, each structural appeal, you whom I address, who cannot change or withdraw or vanish, the whole chain of which, O you whatever your apparatus is for, a link once there that cannot be an instrument of belonging or repetition or by contrast perfectly adequate

5.

Pope John Paul II's coffin emblazoned with the letter M, as those of you may remember, the lights on in the corner papal apartment his last night on Fox News, his devotion to the Virgin Mary, a girl about the same age as Dante's Beatrice, Beatrice "Bice" Di Folco Portinari, with "emerald eyes" and "ineffable courtesy" as shown in every single painting of teenage Mary's sidelong glance when Angel Gabriel tells her she's pregnant, *as if*

6.

Permanent long-ago local boxers on the undercard posing
with their fists for a return, posing with the shot of their life
for a purse whoever else might have a taste, the short-take
denunciation of long-haul financials, my heart which is about
the size of a fist, and the stated Catholic belief that "Those who
follow the stations will not be lost"

7.

Wet cocktail napkins crumpled and stained like the Gowanus
Canal in Brooklyn, its emerald green industrial waste sheen
describing the eyes of Dante's Beatrice as if the Gowanus
Canal could forget an oceanic time of static meditation on sins
committed through no fault of its own just by being brought
into this Brooklyn of miraculous Brooklyn light reflected
off Neptune's ocean beyond the Verrazano-Narrows bridge
suspended like the open wall of Mary's apartment

8.

The world as will and representation of Mary's emerald eyes as
she stares at the floor of her apartment which is always depicted
open to the sky like a boxing ring "in which surely one thing
cannot become another thing having once entered a series of
grounds and consequences, or withdraw from this series" and
vanish into the thin air of the Netherlands on silvery ice skates,
blades slashing across frozen canals, eye just slits in all that glare

9.

Malta, emerald isle in the mind of Muhammad, where Paul, Paul of Melite, "Sits Out Crisis " according to *The Boston Globe* (April 12, 2010) with an "Irish bank's ex-CEO" on the Irish Catholic desert of Cape Cod, his arrest and flight absconding with funds from Jerusalem "to finance the Mandarin Oriental Hotel and the sale of Fan Pier on the South Boston waterfront" whose countless financial instruments are sand in the mind of Muhammad

10.

My devotion to Mary is because I don't remember her asking for or in some way willing any of this stuff, ringed in a neutral corner of her apartment under the glare of Caravaggio's emerald movie spot, its canvas floor our infinite and countless Catholic desert, a blend of Muhammad's desire for Dutch canals and wet cocktail napkins, a publicity shipwreck for Pope Benedict XVI on his visit to Malta—and let's not forget Mary was just a kid—what one Irish economist writing about the green light given to Irish banks and the Catholic Church radiantly calls "the Celtic Chernobyl," my soul's real estate company "which no longer appears to be located at the Boston office where it is listed"

DOWN NEW
UTRECHT AVENUE

1. The Veteran in a New Field (after Winslow Homer)

Sweeping down and across, fingers hooked, countless children
of God calling for another strike, a degree of necessity in
consequence of belonging, a perfectly adequate chain, an
instrument of belonging

Links once there that cannot change or vanish or withdraw,
simple faith licensed to take the meanings that we love, a three-
game series raveling and unraveling the hajj of things drifting
through you

The foreground blurred in what has already become straw
although it has to be too soon for such a change to have occurred
even when it's true that if something is going to become
something else it is already that, a field in which his arms swing
down and across his chest, fingers hooked

Standing in the swale of a 3-2 count, a link once there which
cannot change or withdraw or vanish, a degree of knowledge and
repetition added to illuminate still-living straw blown out of the
frame and countless children of God in the mind of Muhammad

2. Bernie Madoff

Without something like the Catholic Church to stick through time in which a 40% return on investment is unrecurrable unless you have near eternal machinery to elevate you above apartments along New Utrecht Avenue and lighted windows of the D train in the middle of the night, invisible, unknowable in the middle of Brooklyn and the mind of God

Free of everything except character, expectation and desire, a perfectly adequate chain, links that cannot change or vanish or withdraw, the extent of things sifting through you

I can't tell you exactly what it sounded like when the elevated train pulled into the 50th Street station during *Johnny Carson* in the middle of summer with all the windows open, but what I heard was a night-shift union archangel shredding New Utrecht Avenue, asbestos-lined brake-shoes on metal wings, and me with my unmoved Annunciation Mary face in the blue TV light

What a great big world of glorious shit! Ed McMahon shouting *Hey-O!* into the night and tracks in the air above New Utrecht Avenue

3. Holland, or the Netherlands

An oasis in the middle of night, TV stars in care of isolate dreams requisite in desert ways, and the olive green eyes of Mary on her flight into Egypt "to live where fire burnt, also"

Red Sox grounds crew duneing up the pitcher's mound, running outside the base path over wet grass to comb clay for better footing

Flawless execution, like the June Taylor dancers on *Jackie Gleason*.

AWAY

Devoted fan of songsters from Schubert and Cole Porter to Jay-Z and Lady Gaga, and who never fully claimed a fabulous although difficult to detail childhood endowment, death was announced. "Zodiacs of desire once scaffolded that sky," a spokesman said. Marriage earned the nickname "Echo from a wishing well," and children were described as "Mexico to life's Minnesota." Arrangements have not been disclosed. "Some early hopes went up in flames faster than a covered bridge in Exeter, New Hampshire," said one business partner, adding "But shiny as good teeth on a tanned and summer Cape Cod afternoon was their start." Homes followed in the wake of life's bake sales, residences referred to as "Another cardboard box over the steam grate." A foundation called "Exact Spare Change" will be established. Later years saw marbled veins of thicker and some said truer crushed rock whispering under car tires driving up the gravel path. In the city, traffic lights emeralded a soul waiting at the curb. In lieu of flowers, elegant sufficiency, if it have power over blind necessity feastful of clotted gore and contempt of acts of matchless wonder and emptiness—all these shop windows lit up in the early dark to greet you on your way home.

DEAR ALOYSIUS

"Dear Aloysius." He knew without reading further what these words meant. Accepted. Columbia University. Joy flooded his body and mind. He would be the first Cyclops to go to college. With gratitude and sadness he remembered the Jesuit priest who had been marooned on this uncharted island and who offered, along with his books, one simple religion lesson: "Heaven surrounds us like an ocean." New York welcomed him as it did anyone else: without notice. Father Aloysius had taught him well, and he excelled at university, majoring in philosophy. Lack of stereoscopic vision gave him an edge on the varsity pistol team where he earned the nickname "Lighthouse" for his steady aim and marksmanship. Relaxed and gentle, he had lots of dates; female undergrads appreciated what they interpreted as his single attention to them in conversation. His senior-year girlfriend watched as his eyelid closed when they made love. She thought of a stage curtain. She thought, now we can wander offstage. They married after law school. He took a position at one of those Catholic law firms that define the city. He became a sought-after trial lawyer. He and his wife moved to Bay Ridge and had a normal child. On summer evenings he'd put his daughter in her stroller and walk along Shore Road where she tried to catch lightning bugs.

He'd sit on a bench and look at the Verrazano Bridge and the ocean beyond it. His daughter played with fireflies but always rested her final gaze of the evening on her father's broad face. Many years later she flew back from San Francisco with her own family. They walked to the end of the 69th Street fishing pier. She opened a Federal Express overnight plastic sack, took out a handful of silky ash and let it slide into the harbor. Then she upended the sack and they watched as the dark grey silt fell on the water, how it held together for a moment like an island before invisible currents pulled it apart.

THE CATHOLIC CEMETERY IN KAMAKURA

Rice and eel for breakfast and "Fenway Vans Roll to Florida." The roof of Tomoyuki's backyard shed fields plum fungoes off his neighbor's tree. Kevin Youkilis, shown here as a Buddhist monk wiping sweat off his bald baseball of a head, starts for the Red Sox in their Tokyo opener with the Mets. You cannot love against something you know.

The D train unscrolls on a silkscreen in the lobby of the Tokyo Dome Hotel, down elevated tracks above New Utrecht Avenue to Bay Parkway, bamboo bird legs undrawn into their narrow unmotioning bodies. "This is very Japanese," Hiroki Kamata says as he pours beer into my glass just as I am pouring beer into his.

The Bay Parkway stop is a silkscreen panel showing Patty's house, her father a former boxing champ, and a few blocks away, Jay Silverheels, TV's Tonto, is painting an Indian chief's headdress on his front door. Memory unscrolls along elevated tracks above New Utrecht Avenue, and I am drinking Kubota sake at Ya-Ichi in Tokyo with Hiroki and his secretary. In one panel we swap tales about boxing. In another, Hiroki learns English from *The Lone Ranger* on Japanese TV and says he knows Patty's father from old fight films. The next panel shows a waiter rushing in off the street carrying a huge, live crab, and I'm thinking, "Someone's going to enjoy that," and then my surprise when it's brought to our table in a corner of a Japanese prophecy. In the final panel, Hiroki's secretary carefully and secretly peels the label off a bottle of sake. She hands it to me because she is sure I won't remember its name. We leave the restaurant swaying like bamboo as I shout, *Hi-Ho Silver, Away!*

You love against something you cannot know, a funny sort of simple sadness when you think about it, character and fate, memory so ready for it on stretches of the D line above New Utrecht Avenue, blue TV light in apartments watching from the stands.

Your heart is what it is for, says bamboo in the Catholic cemetery in Kamakura.

from TOWARD BLUE PENINSULA

(2014)

RAW YELLOW

A bee stung me on top of my head when I was a kid playing soldiers in Prospect Park, Brooklyn. It left a ping-pong ball size bump my mother saw when I came home.

She made me take a bath.

My mother feared "bugs," anything that flew, crept or crawled. If you lived in a tenement and wanted to keep things nice and not be called shanty Irish, you could see her logic.

One mosquito and she'd pump Flit through our two-room apartment, poison sifting down like it had all the time in the world.

I wasn't in her crosshairs, but, pesticidally speaking, how good can you aim that stuff?

The New York Times said a pesticide called neonicotinoids, nicknamed "neonics" by farmers, is killing bees and raising prices at Whole Foods.

What does it mean when farmers have nicknames for pesticides?

I have a mental defect—probably from all that Flit—where I don't really see or hear what I'm supposed to. I translate for my immediate amusement, a mosquito-thin eternity of private dysfunction too narrow for a chubby bee to enter.

I read neonics as neocons, pleased to turn Cheney and Rumsfeld into poison.

Let's not forget Obama's drones.

Back in college—that big fat hive of blubbery time (which is its solemn gift)—I made peace with bugs. I was tired of swatting, stomping, worrying.

Bugs understood my invisible decision. No longer did they bite me as I lay reading on the summer grass in the backyard on Ash Street, a neighbor's black Lab, named Candy, sleeping next to me, and a bee, now and then, resting on my bare toe.

Bees have cold feet.

And it's something to be young and, you know, just loosely threaded with poison.

VEDONEIRE

A practiced flick of her toe, and dawn shies her champagne lace panties at your head. Could you catch them in your teeth, would it be true enough, felt along the heart, inseparable of grandeur, magnanimity chalked on schoolroom midnight boards, your lagging oath rope heart erased in the sweep of her Stardust chorus girl train? Applause like waves slapping up the side of a lapstrake hull that slipped its mooring to the ends of things?

But they get their due. The calamity of treasures never held much appeal. What did I learn beyond the truth? Now it's for you. O-k-a-y, I might reply, drawing out the "ay" sound like I was asking a question, like, And I'm supposed to do what exactly? I suppose I could say I could "move on" from this, knowing what I discovered. But what's fairly useless in the moment of recognition is what tends to endure, the naturally unfit parts of things I already knew held their value.

Tokens of recognition that chime the naked arm, a wrist so drafty and unbidden. There it is, while something else collapses of its own weight out of sight of this one. Personalize volition or fate for that, why don't ya? And while you're at it, here's an Excel spreadsheet hived with raw data. I'd like each of you to take a cup, cover it with a square of sun-bleached canvas sheeting and place it on a makeshift nightstand along with your leather wallet.

A chain of events, each link the size of a border collie running on ahead to acquire the pendant anchor in whose memory thick canvas sails belled out above the harbor like fine lace scarves drawn around that missing face.

And where did it get you under that banner? Bring me a map made out of straw and if you touch it with the tip of your finger and it begins to burn until no bit of it remains, then I'll believe you, then I'll knot a kerchief around my neck and take my oilskin jacket and wallet and clap you on the back as we climb, shoulder to shoulder, up the gangplank.

THE BOXER AT REST

So, we're square, right? And the answer was a sock in the kisser. I had to admire the skill it was delivered with. Straight jab, enough to rattle my teeth but not cause any real damage. And he wrapped a tea towel around his knuckles twice, closing his fist around the loose ends before he clocked me. That way he didn't hurt his knucklebones and my jaw didn't blossom all black and blue. I did wonder what he was doing with the towel while I waited for an answer: walking over to the rack where the towel was drying, slowly drawing it over the pine dowel beneath the shelf, then wrapping it, as I said, around his half-clenched fist. He even looked like a boxer: bridge of his nose flat as a hairbrush run over by cars all night; his cauliflower ear. Usually I can put two and two together like that.

That's how our lime-green copper and bronze friendship began. Trespass, retribution. No call for outsiders to get involved. No inner remanded forms of repentance and forgiveness. Don't make a federal case out of it. What lingered in the sand-cherry air, lingered. What swept out to sea, swept out like a crate of oranges.

And just as on a floating dock made of long wide planks nailed to grosser beams and held in place by thick wood collars lined with bits of car tires or discarded firehouse canvas hoses to make a loose square around pilings driven deep into the sandy bay floor so the dock can rise or drop with the tide: just so, sea water splashes up between the boards and mixes with the waste of that day's fishing into a liquor of salt water and blood.

There's a kind of covenant with things like ordinary rust or barnacles on pilings driven into the sandy floor of the bay to hide or reveal the truth, whatever blade the face opens to report: a Roman short sword shaped like a frond of New Zealand flax; a blunt oar, hacking at the water like lines from the *Iliad* to get ashore as weather approaches; or feathered over the calm surface of the bay, a soft breeze at play in a pennant atop the main mast, your fists barely clenched around oar handles, the rhythmic chock, chock, chock of wood and oar lock.

Anyway, that's how I saw it, right down to tire marks on the grassy margin where the beach ends and houses like hulls covered in silvery cedar shake huddle near the pier. You walk down the pier to the tavern. On clear nights its casement windows open to salt air; in fog or storm you'd think you were safe aboard a deep-keeled boat. It transformed exactly as you wanted it to, a miracle of place. It was an offering to the gods, or God, or Neptune's trident: straight-backed wooden booths and level tables floating on the foolish tides we carry on. Even the gods, or God, or Neptune enjoyed the glow of liquor bottles arranged in rows on shelves behind the bar. There was ballast in the laughter.

What gets me is, there never was any question in my mind, and I used consequences of actions to plead innocence, as if they were circumstances of cause, a patchwork quilt of Hokusai prints that unscrolled spit-curl waves of prophecy and desire, signs as obvious as if a bronze spit-curl had been inlaid on the side of my head, and when I absent-mindedly tapped it with the edge of a spoon it made a dim, hollow sound like a bell buoy out in the channel that welcomed as it warned away. I tell you, though, that face turned to the side, looking up, head drawn back over the right shoulder, mouth open to breathe, the more to come in the nearness of things.

BREEZY POINT, HURRICANE SANDY

And what was it supposed to be condign? There was no clarity in suffering the low bends or the dearest, no telling what to do apart from it.

To say there was no complicity, narrow slats of wood on a dune fence held together with rusted wire thin as a coat hanger that the sand's slow wave drags down: everyone walked it at a distance knowing what a trial standing in the middle of that mind it would be.

Separated like that, redolent of the smoke of actions they took to secure their place, rushing to save others in parts where things like that happened, and to survive the routine collapse of someone else's life: let's face it, it made them happy in their joinery, salvaged wrecks braving overturned hulls to the ocean.

Smoke did not drift far from that roof. To every surface salt air lent tooth and expectation, things rising and falling in the world, and the choral ode of the waves.

No surprise if you spent your day fighting fires, you'd want to live by the water; if you spent your day hacking through walls and roofs, you'd have a taste for rebuilding driftwood cottages; if you spent your day racing through thick and filthy streets to rescue strangers at the risk of your own life that you'd want seclusion, isolation among your own kind, a prize that you had earned.

Driving past Floyd Bennett Field, over the Marine Parkway Bridge, between Jamaica Bay and the Atlantic Ocean you were safe from the accidents and appearances of things that trapped you between floors.

There could be no equals between a city on fire and a house on the water.

Flooding came first, then fire, opposite of their world which they could not rescue from where they were, doing what they were doing, arrowed way beyond anything they could arrest from the standpoint of origins settled by popular acclaim, waves slapping up the side of a lapstrake hull that slipped its mooring to the ends of things.

Photos in *The New York Times* of houses with weathered sand-colored roofs in choral odes surrounding a blackened burned-out patch like a design for a quilt showing mussels in Caravaggio helmets marshaled on a rock when the tide is out and you can walk among the mysteries of a hidden world turned up.

Mary's sea blue robe draped in waves over her outspread arms like some boxers do; her face, neither absolving nor harrowed, looking down, listening at the more to come in the nearness of things (*NY Times* photo, November 16, 2012).

JERRY LEWIS AT THE PROSPECT

Phil Francini's *Sea Hound* had a broad-beamed lapstrake hull, a small cabin forward of the wheelhouse with two bunks and a head. A fishing boat, its cabin was stowage for tackle: fish hooks of all sizes stuck into the sides of the cabin within easy reach; skeins of tangled fishing line; rusted and shiny reels; rods with missing eyelets; tools of all kinds in an organic, knowing confusion, more like a colony of creatures called "tools" with a life of their own. Double-strapped cushions that were supposed to serve as life preservers had lost their color and buoyancy, streaked with salt water like tide lines.

It was what I thought of as a real boat, broken as the ocean, what a boat would be like on the sea floor, not as a wreck, but as part of that depth.

Phil had been a boxer. His cauliflower ear showed he fought many matches, undercard bouts, without real talent or ambition to take it outside Brooklyn, but he earned enough money and "knew people" for a down payment on a waterfront bar. Before computerized bar tabs, men (always men) put a twenty on the bar, and the price of a drink was taken out along the way. Phil had a switch under the bar and when he threw it the lights went out. "It's OK, just another blackout," he'd calmly reassure everyone, sweeping his thick forearm across the bar top in the dark with all those loose bills, not for the money but for the laugh it gave him when he told my father the next day.

It was the first time I saw how men moved on a boat at night. My father worked on the Brooklyn docks and was always eager to get home early after work, even on weekends when he and Phil went out on the *Sea Hound*. One Sunday, late afternoon, they heard a call on the ship-to-shore. The voice coming through the radio sounded rusted and pitted with salt. My father asked me if I wanted to come along to tow the other boat in. I said yes because I felt too young (third grade, Holy Family Grammar School, now a co-op building) and here was a chance to feel older although the towing took a long time and it was getting late and I was sure I would be out all night and miss the first day of school next morning. How young my father looked in the dark, moving slowly with power and ease.

School had started and I was anxious about skipping a grade: the smallest boy in first grade now more smallest in third, except for Christopher Walsh from Breezy Point. We'd compare our water blisters from the first really good sunburn, then pop them in class and watch our salty body fluids slowly darken our white uniform shirts.

And Jerry Lewis was going to appear in person at the RKO Prospect movie theater on 9th Street in Brooklyn (now a condo building). Jerry Lewis in my neighborhood, my movie theater, its two overhanging balconies, loge seats (whatever they were) that were always closed, and we knew never to go to the toilets up there. There were urinals in the lobby, next to the candy counter. Potato sticks, Nonpareils, popcorn, Jujubes, Juicy Fruits, Good and Plenty, Malt Balls, all in a lighted vitrine. We were candy ourselves to the gods or God or the figure of Neptune on the 4th Ave. bathhouse.

I knew Jerry Lewis from TV specials and him guesting on variety shows, usually his typewriter bit or the spaz routine with a sentimental ending. But this was going to be him, live on stage some time during a pause in *The Ladies Man*, and I wanted to see him go crazy like on TV, with the running and the climbing, with the turning his face to the crowd, with the breaking of the *fla-ay-vin* fourth wall.

And I shouted *There he is!* standing on my plush red movie seat, and all us kids started screaming with anticipation, but it wasn't him and my leg got caught in the folding seat and I was afraid the matron would throw me out before I saw him for real, my leg stuck in the chair like it was the giant clam in *20,000 Leagues Under the Sea*, and all of us shouting and laughing and drowning in the dark.

from THE SINATRA N

(2016)

Such thought, that in it bound
I need no other thing
Wound in mind's wandering,
As mummies in the mummy-cloth are wound

"ALL SOULS NIGHT"
W.B. YEATS

Heraus in eure Schatten, rege Wipfel
Des alten, heil'gen, dichtbelaubten Haines,
Wie in der Göttin stilles Heiligthum
Tret' ich noch jetzt mit schauderndem Gefühl,
Als wenn ich sie zum erstenmal beträte
Und es gewöhnt sich nicht mein Geist hierher.

IPHIGENIE AUF TAURIS
JOHANN WOLFGANG VON GOETHE

In the shadow of your waving treetops, into this sacred, leafy place I
step now as I did then, still devoted, my body shuddering as if for the
first time, and my ghost wasn't here then.

TRANSLATION/ADAPTATION, ED BARRETT

DESIRE, EXPECTATION, IGNORANCE, NECESSITY

Late in his career, because he couldn't hold the note, Sinatra pressed down hard on words ending in n or d, like *and*. He'd find them in the line before the end verse. It was a weird moment, the song suspended and thinking. Something flawed, unsingable let in.

The body fails and we fail in it. The body dies and we die along. Losing faith is a hard thing. Finding faith is a hard thing too. Maybe faith makes life open up. Maybe something new, yet recognizable and expected because desired and hoped for, is revealed. Maybe you become a kind of detective who won't accept a trackless world unmeaning or innocent when there's so much you think you're on to.

He'd slide off the n into the final word in the lyric, suave and natural as a line in Latin by Horace justifying how things turned out for Rome, the Rat Pack at the *Sands* in concert, transforming a bolus of veal and martinis into a star-studded chemical night.

Sometimes I think about what being religious is like, a body imparlant with God: all paradise local, your loosely threaded carriage through a crowd caught on security cameras.

A needle on a vinyl record unwound a voice inside your head, what you wanted—what you needed—to tell yourself, and *in it bound* you didn't need no other thing, *as mummies in the mummy-cloth are wound*. His sly young voice learning the mechanics of singing into a microphone, metal and wires to pierce a wound and be annealed. Three minutes of tuneful, banal truth, all slipstream draft and emotional fairings, none of the elaborate riggings of operatic fate, those slowly capsizing narrative hulls rolling over with barnacles and sea-grass as tokens of revelation: *"Br-br-brother...?" "Sis-sis-sister...?"* And now that we've all been transfigured, what's left is revenge slaughter, which awakens the step-dog who once innocently sniffed around your crotch, now Eternal Dog Bounty Hunter whose sleeve chain tattoo gets yanked by the less dismal, yet usually not around until later Benign Ones, who, we must have forgotten, were implicated in all this to begin with, and whose intercession now offers redemption as an operating system: if something turns into something else, wasn't it always that, shuddering as if for the first time in your shadow?

What am I supposed to make out of these things exactly? And I do mean *exactly*. I'd like to have instructions and a plot summary to follow along with, please—at least a song somewhere down the line to tell me *What'll I do* even if it whispers *You'll never know if you don't know now.* These are simple objects. I'm an object: fingerprints, DNA, burrs all golden on the gown of being. They belong to me and I am theirs. To what end? In what angle of all the security cameras facing dumbly, saintly, down Boylston Street do I appear and disappear? Standing there on the sidewalk sans script, sans argument, sans words, sans everything you once thought sufficient. *Exit you.*

BOSTON LATIN

An LNG tanker heading up Boston harbor to offload in Everett; trailing-edge ailerons on an Aer Lingus plane in descent to Logan over three-deckers and single-families in East Boston and Winthrop; white waves flaring off the bow of a center-console fiberglass speedboat juiced with twin Honda outboard engines unzipping Massachusetts Bay; downtown condo and office developments, their slender crane masts with aerial wheelhouses moored in landfill along I-93 and the Mass Pike.

The body shuddering, "and my ghost wasn't here then," pleading its case for insufficiency, a chain of events, each link big as a dog's head, a series in which one thing cannot become another thing or withdraw on streets closed off to traffic for the marathon, filled with people who never once doubt the stuff they're made of.

Annunciation Mary is in the middle of her apartment, which is shown open to the air like a construction site. Heads of corollary angels bulb out of the sky like security cameras impassively recording Boylston Street. Mary is holding a book about the size of an iPhone, which distracts her because she doesn't notice an archangel standing right next to her, his robes painted bright as a State Trooper's high-vis jacket on traffic duty. She is still a child by state law. A ray like a syringe pierces her body, targeted, precise as an MRI at Mass General.

Do the big cries ever wear themselves out, improbable as coming back to life in a country full of windmills, their sails facing heaven in a grammar of endings?

And the Constitution of the Commonwealth of Massachusetts has already been signed, and all its articles displayed, for each of us to accept at the price of being protected by them anyway. It's Boston and it's still winter. Laws that state we have a natural right to be what we have always been sound astonishingly true like oracles, promising, as gods do in oracles, one thing we think, when, really, we learn in exile something else. "Well, at least we were able to talk with them," I suppose you could say in Latin. And it translates back into you, sifting through you, a daily tide of going out for things and coming back in, the whole astute mess stepping disabused onto the street again.

BLOW-IN ADDRESSES

(2021)

My neighbor John Kennedy in Dunquin, Co. Kerry, received a grant from the Irish Government to record forgotten field names in the small Irish-speaking village of Dunquin, the most westerly in Ireland, where my family home is. Names are given in Irish and English.

BÓITHRÍN AN PHROPERTY
ROAD OF THE PROPERTY

I'm a blow-in, so I don't write much about Dunquin because maps are drawn and I respect that. But a lot of things in life just blow in, *being both chance and choice*, my heart *to sink into its own delight at last*, postage stamp fields, looking out the window of Aer Lingus Flight 134 Boston to Shannon: Boston that I blew into from Brooklyn where I first blew into this life although my mother was told she couldn't have children and then her sister's abandoned nine-year old boy blew in at her door and then she got pregnant with me. It's not uncommon. "Brooklyn Betty" is the name we give our horse on Race Night at Kruger's pub where one night toward the end of my mother's life we were listening to music and Eddie Campion asked my mother to dance. She rested her cane against the corner bench, got up and danced. She loved to dance in a life that didn't promise much dancing. You never know. After twenty-five years our house is still called *Tigh Tom na Inise*, Tom Ó Dálaigh, Tom of the Island, *na*, "of," one of those prepositional phrases we live in, language and thought in a syntax of dependencies that decline recognition in a grammar of things. Tom Hutch said my name comes up as "Dunquin Yank" on his mobile. We laughed about that. As if these names, we were theirs to know, and they did know us for ourselves alone.

AN DROICHEAD BÁN
THE WHITE BRIDGE

It's important to ask, now and then, what do I really love? It's a simple question. Things change, you change. Count what you would never want to depart from you, an accounting limited by the number of knuckles on your right hand, hard as stone under your shifting skin.

NA CLUAINTEACHA DUBHA
THE DARK MEADOWS

Not to be loved is a hard thing, unimaginable to anyone who has "a love in their life." Hard not ever to have shared a nature, your nature, distinct from capital N nature, the once-in-a-lifetime "you," maybe not "the best of..." but certainly what you feel, and therefore know, to be "the only" "... of all possible worlds"—your world, your day-to-day life and labor, and the hilarity, for lack of a better word, you feel sometimes when it's like you're on a boat in a following sea, waves traveling in the same direction you are, the staggering liquor of life digging you in and under.

GLEANN NA BPÚCAI
GLEN OF THE FAIRIES

This afternoon, on the centenary of The Rising, I read a quote by Roger Casement who was explaining our rights which he described as "a thing born in us at birth," and I was wondering why "born in us" had to be explained further as "at birth." A little later I was looking out my kitchen window, doing the dishes, looking at our little bit of field and the ocean beyond it, wondering about Casement's phrasing, mindlessly noticing that I had two bottles of dish-washing liquid on the sink. One was SuperValu and had the word *Apple* on the label. The other was Fairy Liquid which had *Apple Orchard* on the label. I guess Fairy Liquid is more expensive because SuperValu (€0.79) was just an apple, but Fairy Liquid (€1.50) is the whole orchard. I thought, who wants a plate to smell like apples? Out of what vat of chemical natures was this apple scent plucked? I was thinking about what's born in us and when it gets born in us if not at birth. I liked the idea of things being born in us as life goes on, as, say, an apple tree ripens outside a chemical plant. "At birth" is too soon to be defined by things, although of course maps are drawn. But everything and always? The field I'm looking at wasn't born in me and I wasn't born in it. But I carry it around in me now. It bears what I do with it. What if I planted an apple tree? What if I planted a whole orchard, its scent blowing in through this open window, natural, uncapturable except as dish-washing liquid? My apple thoughts pass over this field and the field doesn't beep like the checkout counter at Garvey's supermarket when the cashier sweeps my bottle of Fairy Liquid over the laser. What's "born in us at birth" that has *super valu*, blown in from God knows who or where, if God or apple-scented fairies have anything to do with it?

BÓITHRÍN NA MARBH
ROAD OF THE DEAD

We're all just a bunch of ghosts walking around on our stupid legs anyway, waiting for, *y'know*, because if something is going to turn into something else, isn't it always that? Animals in a field eye us and think, "Why are they always standing on their hind legs? That's got to be a difficult balancing act, not to mention a waste of energy when it's so much easier using all four legs. And their snouts so far above the ground up there like that. How can they tell what anyone is thinking? And why do they always smell like apples?"

AN MÚCHÁN
UNDERGROUND PASSAGE

I was looking at the ocean over this patchwork quilt of fields. It was late winter, and ocean night was flooding the fields, a colder night than I expected, and when I slid my body under my patchwork quilt, shuddering at the touch of cold sheets, my body a bit of turf, its slow dark radiance, and the ocean dreaming me into itself.

CAOLÓG AN GHLEANNA
NARROW FIELD OF THE GLEN

Drawn on a map, these fields look like a sheet of postage stamps lying flat in a kitchen drawer you've opened looking for a pair of scissors or loose string. Or they're C5 envelopes, not the self-sealing or peel-and-seal kind, but the kind you lick with the tip of your tongue, the last place the soul leaves the body when you die.

DROICHEAD AN GHLINN DEIRG
ROAD OF THE RED GLEN

(path to stream where older women washed clothes)

There's a lot I don't know. I don't know if Saoirse Ronan is a good actor, for example. It's hard to tell if a story, moving like a ghost in and through time, makes an actor good because the story is bigger than the actor, coming before the actor, inhabiting the actor, as Roger Casement might say, a story we know, or, hearing it for the first time, recognize it as our own. Or does an actor, Saoirse Ronan for example, offer a field of being that captures one of these ghosts moving in and through us, making it real again, young and stupid again, kids laughing and throwing pebbles at an old woman standing in a stream?

GORT ON UISCE
FIELD OF WATER

A canvas-wrapped hull upside down over the heads of three men walking it to the pier like a beetle about to burrow underground where another ocean floats our thin scratch of earth, moist as birthday cake.

BÓTHAR CHÉILLEACHAIR
KELLIHER'S ROAD

I am thinking of Main Campion. I am thinking of the post office in her house. I am thinking of the scale she used to weigh my letters back to the States. I am thinking of the brass weights she used for the scale. How much can a single envelope weigh, and how did *An Post* create such a small brass weight for that? I miss stamps printed with harps or wrens without computer bar scans. I miss licking the stamp. I miss the candies and groceries she sold from behind the counter in the post office, how she'd come out of her sitting room, unfold the post office counter-leaf like opening a big map, all these kids clutching pennies to buy sweets.

ABHAINN AN GHLINN DEIRG
RIVER OF THE RED GLEN

John Kennedy raised bees along the side of this river in a spot hidden by fuchsia bushes not far from the road on the Russell plot. No one walking along the road would think, "I bet that dark bend in the river has a hive buzzing with tireless worker bees, a queen bee swollen with generations waiting their turn, a civilization constructing itself, relatively at peace until disturbed, although probably at bee-war against other hives." It's not a common thought unless you are a beekeeper. I think—and this is probably a moral judgment on my part— most people are afraid of bees and don't seek them out. I used to have the same fear, but many years ago I was lying on the grass, reading a book, and fell asleep. I was awakened by a tickling feeling on my big toe. A bee had landed there, moving its legs the way bees do to gather pollen. Tough luck bee, I thought. I didn't brush it off because I was groggy and it amused me and because I was surprised at how cold bee feet felt. I lost my fear of bees right then and there. And I apologize to beekeepers everywhere for saying this, but I think bees in honeycomb shelves look like hot buttered popcorn when you're rushing to pay before the movie starts.

TIGH DEAN NEACHTAIN
DAN NAUGHTON'S HOUSE

(from Galway)

from Galway and the River Corrib, its braid of locks thick as
letter-knuckled Irish written on the page, all slide and elision
on the tongue.

GARRAITHE DEAIN
DAN NAUGHTON'S GARDENS

The Corrib in flood under my daughter Ciara's third floor window above Bridge Street is the world crashing through the world, bare-knuckled Conor McGregor, Ireland's Ultimate Fighting Champion, telling *The Irish Times*, "We're all human here at the end of the day, regardless of color, gender, sexuality. We all deserve the same rights."

TOBAR DHUALACH
NATURAL WELL

Not entire of it, not entire myself, something temporary for
something permanent, a tongue underground of water.

AN CLOIGEANN
END OF TOWNLAND

Each map a canopy over the field you find yourself contained in for the moment, about now, when you're ill-informed about the nature of the struggle each one of us must endure, or even that there has to be a struggle, starting now, and later, all along: how contrasts linger, the clarity absorbs those first trivial, immense relationships, how in each were honor and misfortune. And the face hidden throughout? It was your own likeness in the fields that day, a lingering clarity the contrasts absorb, how the story had sought no one.

BÓITHRÍN NA MARBH

for William Corbett

There's a narrow grassy path that rises from the Dunquin harbor to the foot of the surrounding hills. It's called *Bóithrín na Marbh* in Irish, which is translated as "Road of the Dead." *Bóithrín* is Irish for "road," but any adult standing in the middle of this grassy path could reach their arms out and touch the montbressia flowers and fuchsia hedges that line it on both sides. So this bóithrín is more a "lane" than a "road," the same width as the Mass. Ave. bike lane in Cambridge between Harvard Square and MIT. If you swim in a pool, it's as wide as a lane for doing laps. Blasket Islanders, who lived on *An Blascaod Mór*, "the Great Blasket," an island three miles off the coast of Dunquin, used this lane when they rowed a currach carrying a coffin cradling the dead from the island to the Dunquin pier for burial in the graveyard on the mainland. When I look out to the Blasket Island from my kitchen window in Dunquin, the island's silhouette resembles a cow resting on its side in a field. Islanders would walk the road of the dead in a single line behind the coffin. They also walked the Blasket Island's narrow path along its steep cliffs in a line because the cliffs are sheer, wet and slippery. It was not uncommon that an islander would fall to a prevailing death, so walking one behind the other along the road of the dead was nothing new. I wonder if any of the islanders, when they accompanied their dead through this lane and brushed against the montbressia with its fiery orange blossom tongues, and the fuchsia with its hanging red petal bells, if they saw this abundance of nature within reach as a celebration of life. Or did it feel like a rebuke of their own once-in-a-lifetime life, we who are part of nature, but different? The road of the dead cuts through privately owned fields. Land in Ireland has always been sacramental, "an outward sign of an inner grace"—the fanatic heart, Yeats called it—its image and its cause. But Dunquin locals whose fields are divided by this lane don't object to this weirdly straight ditch through their land. The lane isn't used for pulling the dead off the sea anymore: it's a shortcut from the top of the village, where I live, to the lower, harboring pub. I don't walk through Bóithrín na Marbh because its grass is always wet, and I don't like standing in a pub in wet shoes and jeans. If you do laps in a pool, standing in a pub with wet shoes and jeans is the feeling you have when you pull yourself up the ladder as the pool's buoyant embrace slides down your mostly naked body and gravity grabs you around your comically stoic Speedo cresting the surface of the pool. Last summer there was a drought in Ireland. I wanted to tell you how road tar was melting in the sun, how driving through it made a sound like driving through early winter slush on Mass. Ave. I wanted to tell you that our neighbor, when she was a girl, used to stand barefoot on this melting tar because she liked to feel it squishing up between her toes, how her mother got angry when she came home because she had to use butter to clean the tar off. On chilly days, she said she'd go into the field where her cows were resting, push one away, and lie down in the warm circle of grass its body left.

VIKING RENGA

(2022)

VIKING RENGA

for Don Berger

1.

When I was a kid, I used to think ribbons suddenly grew out of my fingers when I was walking. I'd go down the block with my arms spread out like bird wings, trying to keep my ribbons from getting tangled up. I never thought about it, why ribbons grew out of my fingers, why I had to keep them untangled, a kid following in the wake of unwept mouths, dull and cornered by the force of one life among lives with their own force promoted on the promise of some kind of unbalanced awe that will change into the very ground beneath your feet, the familiar made new and solid as a river frozen steel-blade deep, fierce-laced glide and shouts across the moment of contact with something true and immortal in the nearness of things to come.

What are these things when they leave us, or we leave them, and what do I want them to do, what could they do encumbered by intentions, expectations, all those dreams of fate and freedom, two sides of the same desire flipping its coin up in the air, slapped down on the back of a hand reaching out in the air our breath purls through, a background called nature for the everything that's here now, children carried off on deer, wingéd children, on deer with basalt hooves?

161

2.

"...and still the / question was elusive." The question is elusive to brave the passage, the Lucretian slant of sleet coating everything without trying. Nothing missed, wrapped up tight in ice popcorn bubbles, tight as a package from Amazon, even when it's nothing special, without consequence, tracked with clarity about point of origin and current state and eventual arrival. And the moments of its journeyed end, each documented, nothing lost, shared in its passage—shared only because of its passage—something which existed as a thought in ordinary need or flashpoint of want.

3.

"Snow falling only by itself now," as if beyond contoured drama, a stage direction for nothing. Tell me, if you know this, tell me how the audience is behaving on their side of the curtain which, instead of dropping before their eyes, descends upon their upraised faces softly as a kiss, a whisper, "You're the one." You are the one, the one and only, like everyone else.

And just like that the room got up on its heels and left a contour of the room empty as snow that's fallen all night in the luxurious blur of things that can't dream. It is their undreamt dreams we live inside of, under a sky all scumbled with scudding clouds.

I wouldn't mind playing the star. Not a diva in a Jujube sprinkly tux outside the movie theater being paparazzied, photographers shouting "Here, over here" like drowning crew members in the wake of my galleon whose sails bay out saltily in the sky, calling for rescue. They "perish'd each alone." But being special is something I think we all want now and then, maybe not as a fulltime career, smooth as motor oil leaking from the lips of George Sanders' voice so in love with its own sound, a spring sliding over slate grey stones, undiminished until by some curse that stars live only so long as they don't recognize themselves, and they do, as they must, as anyone must.

Rungs on a ladder burnished a bright beer color by all the hands that have held on and were violently stripped away, or silently unfurled: The staved-in cries of desire dance their small loves. But does it count? Who would say, "Oh, it's still ticking over, it's fine and, well, parallel, if you know what I mean," and not hope for it to converge somewhere down the line after the station recedes into nothing, into the background which reduces it to an invisible dot-size cup of oblique, intractable gravity and fate waiting for you at the next stop, all waves and tears.

One thing turns into another thing, "exhaling wings" in a language shiny and new as an arrow made from hard ash, breath and words the body and blood of an arrow that draws its curse back along a line to the crook'd arm, hand even with nipple, steady aim, intent blind to the invisible truth in a drizzle of rust and laughter.

And birds recoiled. They formed an air cap over Boston when it was growing up. That's obvious. But they got lost, and who wrote back "Yes, so far we're okay," words that cut across the sky and—you maybe guessed it—started to rain.

4.

Daffodil blades knifing through the confused late winter river bank of the Charles. This is a start of rigging for schooner spring and spinnaker summer, sails baying out saltily, full throated sea chanteys and dancing on deck even though right now it feels more like building a ship inside a bottle. Where do they get this stuff, all those aerial strings and pulleys?

My eyes aren't running out of sight and I like the outside world more than the inside world. There's more stuff to see, even small stuff, my laces slowly coming undone when I'm walking which I follow with enough interest to learn how long those loops will hold on until I have to genuflect on one knee to pull them up and begin the ritual again. I don't think I learn anything from that, but it is what I do every time my laces come undone if I'm in no danger of tripping over them. I don't think I learn anything about myself, which would be weird if I did, right there at my feet, right there on the ground.

Seeing Clown Construction Company instead of Crown Construction Company, is one of those Intimations of Immortality moments I get great pleasure from, when what I see is not what is there, it's what I want, and it makes life more like life and is therefore a kind of oblique immortality, an immortality on curfew: like, OK, here's a brief glimpse of those golden ellipses "felt in the blood and felt along the heart" dot dot dot. There's more to say, but you get the main idea, "simple faith / Licensed to take the meaning that we love." But a construction company for crowns, or even for clowns whose art is all about timing, wouldn't be in business for long if it allowed for tolerances that loose in its products, faith actually licensed to take any meaning that we love. Anything? I suppose that's how things work, anyway. And what product are we looking for? Where do you look for it? "Go to all the churches in Boston" and eavesdrop on insufficiency on its knees offering up a heart which is about the size of a fist or a big yellow lemon.

I went to Ikea in Stoughton, Mass., because a fire was in my head for kitchen cabinets. This place is bigger than an aircraft carrier. And I am lost. I told the customer service person whose hair she dyed an apple blossom red, I am lost. Shayna helped me find my way. That's a nice ring, I said to pass the immortality-time an image took to load on her laptop, is that a Celtic design? I am Irish and Scottish, she said of her research on Ancestry.com where we go to find ourselves or some little silver trout of ourselves, and hook a berry to a thread, some little sliver to squeeze through into the kitchen joinery of history and justice and truth invoked by a name who now calls out to you by name.

5.

"These are the loveliest hours, until one adjusts oneself," says Ernie Kovacs about early evening in the movie *Five Golden Hours*. I like that halting affirmation of nature, or nature's beauty, and a suspicion of it, of getting lost in something that's all background to the moment and the skin we're in. "Good morning nature, you want to kill me," was poet Robin Blaser's aubade. Same double vision. Coleridge thought human nature completed what I guess I have to call impersonal nature—inhuman nature—and gave voice to its mute, indecipherable expression of . . . I forget of what, "this sweet cesspool" actor George Sanders called it in his suicide note, "And when I went away," John Clare wrote in "The Mouse's Nest," "the water o'er the pebbles scarce could run / And broad old cesspools glittered in the sun."

All the churches in Boston have statues to crab saints. Sermons are delivered from pulpits in the shape of blue-claw crabs, their claws reaching out to capture or embrace. As a kid, I thought blue-claw crabs were "better looking" than other crabs for some reason, their claws extended as they waited on pilings near the knife-gouged wood table on the pier where I used to swim in polluted tides, the day's catch, scaled, sliced open, guts thrown into the bay, blue-claw crabs waiting, their claws blue as my eyes.

6.

But the sky won't stop. Why should it, up there in the sky like that? Would I if I were like that? But I'm not like that. It's there, day and night, and who doesn't shoot arrows through it to something else above it or outside it, something it's hiding: prayers, curses and cries exhaling our arrows.

Doesn't it feel like the soul—assuming it exists somewhere inside where it floats around with everything else in there— or it's what that inner you is floating in—not inner like true or the real secret you one reflects on sometimes—but small pulleys and silvery cables (a ship within a bottle sort of thing), your lapstrake ribs and riggings: like the body is like a hull full of sea water, maybe in a following sea where the boat's going in the same direction as the waves which wash over the deck and submerge it in the sea right up to the gunwales, and what it had been sailing on it is now equal to.

Such conditions are endless, they don't arrive one after the other like missionaries or Vikings pulling their shallow-draft hulls up on the shore, held fast with braided lines of thick rope drying in the sun. That's one example fate has up its draping haute couture sleeve, its nimble sewing and attention to detail mostly unrecognizable because this sort of workmanship takes pride in knowing what it knows and doesn't look outside itself for approval, secure in anonymity.

Like so, so many arrivals on time that are no longer around,
begins our epic in perfect dactylic hexameters stretched out on
the grass. It holds a space for you to lie down next to it, staring
at the clouds moving in their determined way, like there was
some intent, like they know what will happen, secrets that
eventually get out, whispered in the grass. The sky is wearing
eyeliner and its shoulders are bronze under spaghetti straps
because the day is still young and charming and can dress
like nothing was more easily discovered than truth, nothing
apparent that was not what it really was, nothing that wasn't
itself alone.

"Oh, well, alright, I'm with you on this now." I really do say
that to myself, not a talking-to-myself behavioral problem,
but a conscious decision to wade out into spring, which
doesn't care who accedes to mortality: "no action needs to
be taken" is its carefree wave hello, the pre-checked box that
keeps me on this eternal email list. My identity, some chunk of
it, has already been stolen by an A.I. bot using "All are / naked
none is safe" software code, known acronymically in chummy
programming language as "AaNNiS," pronounced "Annie's,"
human and relatable, definitely not asking for personal info.

Something to say to the person one loves: "You are my
language." This is a very direct statement about how that
person describes life for them now, not just rhetoric's squirrels
twerking up and down tree trunks and across pendant
branches with their magnificent small claws. It's not a

weighted fishing lure with a hook hidden inside its life-like cast. It's really more like history's Achilles' heel, all the small cries, unacknowledged, or sometimes something that's just what you want. And when that sentence ends with a panache of three rhetorical dots hiccupping either toward something everyone knows, or something totally unexpected, but now we see that it was always following us in torn rags and clumsy cothurni…

7.

Act Two opens with a partial sun going wobbly in a mix-up and a slice of Boston cream pie holding up space, all of space, even the meaningless parts astronomers are so lovey-dovey about. One of their candle-lit telescopes enters stage right, a real *coup de théâtre* for its spectacle (the telescope is disguised as "Night") and for its monologue—an aria really—as the telescope reveals it's the ghost of a ship's hull that had capsized before this play begins, as the birthday boy pretends to blow out candles on his cake.

Memory is fate, as if you hadn't noticed. I always thought of it as an active search organ somewhere inside the mind. "The mind" is where it lives, even though *mind* is beginning to feel like an over-hyped, long-in-the-tooth celebrity whose photo is always featured on the cover of the checkout aisle mag *Things You Think You Know*, a thing you could follow on Instagram. Memory takes note of some things and not other things; and if it is just passively impressed by something dramatic that's outside of you, as happens all the time, it absorbs that to nourish its main job, keeping the tracks clear of debris so that the train "comin' down the track" arrives on schedule. Its arrival time, however, is unposted, but the screen shows it's "on time" on a track number "to be announced." The rails have been laid, squiggly as a plate of linguini with traction, not a single strand slipping off the tines of your eager fork.

Boston stage directions for today: scene changes to very sunny; UV warnings and SPF 40 sunscreen recommendations noted in weather app; high pollen count; very warm, almost 80 degrees; State House crowd protesting leaked Supreme Court draft reversing Roe v. Wade. Exit nothing. Enter everything. Chorus mills. Faint ripple through scrim made of salt from ocean breeze offstage.

Imaginary boundary lines float in rivers and oceans, digital GPS coordinates, accepted invisible lines, like the fishy, squimmy middle of the Charles River which in its polluted, heron obsessed way divides Cambridge from Allston, Allston which I think is part of Boston, just not the Boston of history and literature, its thoughtfulness chalk marks on midnight classroom boards. *The Boston Globe* reports Sinn Féin's victory in Northern Ireland's parliament elections, *sinn féin*, Irish for *ourselves alone*, imparlant with what?

And let me just say ("let me just say" is a polite way of insisting without any real knowledge), let me just say, we know a lot of things that add on without adding up. The No. 66 bus to Brookline feels like it takes forever. So many times when the eternal feels this close.

quale [kwa-lay]: Eng. n 1. A property (such as hardness) considered apart from things that have that property. 2. A property that is experienced as distinct from any source it may have in a physical object. Ital. pron.a. 1. Which, what. 2. Who. 3. Some. 4. As, just as.

∮